Cooperative Collection Management

The Conspectus Approach

Edited by
Georgine N. Olson
Barbara McFadden Allen

NEAL-SCHUMAN PUBLISHERS, INC.
New York, London

Published by Neal-Schuman Publishers, Inc.
100 Varick Street
New York, NY 10013

Library of Congress Cataloging-in-Publication Data

Cooperative collection management : the conspectus approach / edited
    by Georgine N. Olson and Barbara McFadden Allen.
        p.   cm.
        Includes bibliographical references (p .   ).
        ISBN 1-55570-200-7
        1. Collection development (libraries) -- United States.   2.Library
cooperation--United States .   3. Collection development (Libraries) -
-United States -- Evaluation.   I. Olson, Georgine N.   II. Allen,
Barbara McFadden , 1958-
Z687 . 2 . U6C66 1994
025 . 2 '1 ' 0973 -- dc20   94-20036
                                                         CIP

Contents

Editor's Introductory Note
by Barbara McFadden Allen, Illinois State Library, Springfield, Illinois   5

Theoretical Value of Conspectus-Based
(Cooperative) Collection Management
by Barbara McFadden Allen   7

A CLOSER LOOK AT CONSPECTUSES
CURRENTLY USED IN U.S. LIBRARIES

RLG & NCIP CONSPECTUS

RLG and NCIP: A Brief Overview and Selected Bibliography
by Barbara McFadden Allen   11

KRUEGER METHOD

The Krueger Method: An Introduction
by Georgine N. Olson, Corn Belt Library System, Bloomington, Illinois   13

Illinois Valley Library System and the
Development of the Krueger Method
by Bill Erbes, Illinois Valley Library System, Pekin, Illinois   15

The Krueger Manuals: A Case Study
by Kimberly Bunner, Parlin-Ingersoll Library, Canton, Illinois   19

Krueger Lives: An Unscientific Exploration
by Georgine N. Olson   25

WLN CONSPECTUS

WLN Conspectus: An Introduction
by Georgine N. Olson   29

The WLN Conspectus
by Sally Loken, WLN, Lacey, Washington   31

Using the WLN Conspectus in a
Non-Automated Environment
by Nancy Powell, Consulting Librarian, Albany, Oregon   43

Shared Futures: Cooperative Collection
Development and Management in Alaska
by June Pinnell-Stephens, Fairbanks North
Star Borough Public Library, Fairbanks, Alaska   57

FICTION ASSESSMENT

Fiction Assessment: An Introduction
by Georgine N. Olson   63

Quality *and* Demand: The Basis for Fiction
Collection Assessment
by Sharon L. Baker, University of Iowa School
of Library Science, Iowa City   65

Designing a Fiction Assessment Tool: The Customer
Service Approach
by Burns Davis, Nebraska Library
Commission, Lincoln   69

Effects of Fiction Assessment on a Rural Public Library
by Marietta Weber, Chatsworth Township
Library, Chatsworth, Illinois   83

THE CONSPECTUS IN (COOPERATIVE) COLLECTION MANAGEMENT

Conspectus as a Tool for (Cooperative) Collection Management
by Georgine N. Olson   87

Employing Collection Management
as an Institutional Change Agent
by Tom Dorst, Illinois State Library, Springfield, Illinois   91

Cooperative Collection Management Among Four Rural Libraries
by Ruth Shasteen, Elizabeth Titus
Memorial Library, Sullivan, Illinois   97

Process to Promise: the CCM Plan
by Brenda J. Foote, Sparta Public Library, Sparta, Illinois   101

Editor's Introductory Note

by Barbara McFadden Allen

In this special, double issue of Neal Schuman's *Collection Building* journal, we bring together a number of diverse articles representing the thinking of a broad spectrum of librarians. The authors contributing to this issue offer a variety of perspectives on the use of conspectus methodology in the assessment of library collections and the use of such assessments in the development of collection management or *cooperative collection management policies.*

We have endeavored, insofar as possible, to offer the reader information about projects which have not been widely publicized. Hence, we offer a cursory review of the RLG conspectus and the North American Inventory Project. Not so much because these projects are unimportant. Far from it. The RLG and NCIP laid the groundwork for much of what is written in this volume. However, rather than offer additional articles on these already well-covered projects, we offer an overview and bibliography.

This collection delves deeper into other conspectus methodologies—particularly the WLN conspectus and the process of fiction assessment. You will find practical articles detailing successful projects in libraries large and small, and you will be treated to several thoughtful considerations of these subjects as they relate to other aspects of library services.

I hope you find this issue helpful and thought provoking.

Barbara McFadden Allen is a Networking Consultant for the Illinois State Library in Springfield.

Theoretical Value Of Conspectus-based (Cooperative) Collection Management

by Barbara McFadden Allen

While approaching the theoretical value of conspectus-based cooperative collection management, I'll address the issues as they relate to resource sharing in general. I'll repeat a number of themes from a number of perspectives so that you may have the opportunity to reflect on these issues, and I'll outline for you some of my personal philosophy on the subject, which I refer to as "the networking imperative." The intent is to issue a call to action, rather than describe the processes associated with cooperative collection management or collection assessment.

I pledge that I will not use the word "paradigm" once, nor will I use the word "impact" as a verb. In return, I ask that you temporarily set aside any personal concerns you may have about cooperative collection management as it applies to your specific institution. I ask you to view these issues first in the broadest possible sense, and consider how these issues effect our profession as a whole.

Much has been written of late on the benefits of "access versus ownership" of library materials. Whole religions seem to be springing up among librarians devoted to the worship (or denigration) of interlibrary loan, bibliographic access, document delivery, and/or other variations on this theme. The underlying premise being that in an environment of restricted budgets and inflationary pricing of monographs and serials, access, to and delivery of, materials held outside the confines of a single institution takes on an expanded role in the delivery of services to the library user.

Recently described as a "crisis in acquisitions," the age-old problem of the inability to meet all local needs with local collections is cited as the most compelling reason to review current thinking on this subject, and indeed, statistical evidence abounds[1] indicating that individual libraries are experiencing a rather dramatic reduction in the ability to purchase materials at previous levels. This plethora of data—overwhelming in scope—compels us to examine the relationships between the related activities of collection management, material delivery, bibliographic access, and traditional interlibrary loan.

Profound changes must occur in the ways we collect information, disseminate information, and how we budget for those activities. However, effective cooperation must be based on human interaction among and between the libraries affected. As an example, I'd like to take a look at the issues associated with the broad bibliographic access now afforded to virtually anyone with a personal computer, a phone line, and a modem.

VIRTUAL LIBRARY: OUR PATRONS BELIEVE IT'S HERE...DO YOU?

The virtual library, which is fundamentally electronic access to a universe of library collections and materials from a desktop, may place even greater demands on our collections. The problem with the belief that the virtual library

Barbara McFadden Allen, issue co-editor, is Networking Consultant at the Illinois State Library, Springfield, Illinois.

has arrived, and the complacency towards addressing further development, is that there is no standard for delivery of information through virtual access.

In fact, the issue may not solely concern the gap between what is published and what has been purchased. The enhanced bibliographic access available not only to librarians but to all users of such mega-systems (i.e., the Internet), requires each institution to gain physical access to those items which have been identified through this bibliographic access. Libraries serve an increasingly sophisticated population which may now request known items that have been identified through online searching. We could define this as the ever-widening gap between what users know to be available and what is owned locally.

Within this context, the most effective model for the virtual library of the future consists of individual institutions with shared bibliographic databases joining forces to develop policies for the cooperative development and management of these shared collections, cooperative electronic bibliographic access to the collections, and cooperative delivery of the materials on demand. Working together, these institutions can then reach out in an ever-broadening circle to more and more institutions, each sharing a commitment to build collections that meet local needs, while supporting the needs of other institutions in this network. Make no mistake, the foundation of this kind of activity remains, as before, cooperative policy development founded on individual, human commitments to the development and maintenance of services.

In turn, the foundation for such policy development is an understanding of local practice—an understanding which can be fostered through the process of assessment. In my opinion, it appears that user demands for enhanced access or delivery of services may be met with demands from the library—that the users pay for these services. Too often, librarians misinterpret the call to become more "entrepreneurial" and "businesslike" as a call to charge fees. I'll return to the subject of assessment in a moment, but first I'd like to examine how assessment is specifically related to this call for a more "businesslike" environment in library administration.

FEES FOR SERVICE OR BETTER MANAGEMENT THROUGH ASSESSMENT?

Within the private sector, a business concern that did not periodically review its products and services in light of consumer demand might soon find itself out of business. Successful concerns, large and small, generally thrive in an environment in which they find their "niche," or they continue to change and modify product and service offerings to keep up with the capricious demands of a diverse consumer group. Oddly enough, many libraries and other public agencies have not reacted the same way to consumer needs. Arguably, steady and consistent funding sources may have caused us to become complacent. Nonetheless, the market forces of consumer demand effect all of us working in libraries, public or private. What's more, citizens, governing boards, as well as administrative and government agencies are joining the common call of accountability. Fundamentally, libraries of all types, regardless of source of funding or mission, exist to provide access to, and delivery of, information on demand—information that is often hand selected by staff and made available to the public as the existing combination of collections and services.

Rather than rush to charge fees, perhaps ignoring the problems of diverse demands and static budgets along the way, we may choose to analyze existing products (collections) and services (access) more carefully. The process of collection assessment provides a fundamental tool for the management of the growth (in both depth and breadth) of the library's collection. Assessment provides us an opportunity to review "where the library has been" and can serve as the basis for building a roadmap for the future—a business plan, if you will.

COLLECTION ASSESSMENT: THE OPPORTUNITY TO DEFINE OURSELVES

The process of collection assessment provides data which can be useful in both a local and a cooperative context:

1. Collection data generated through the process of assessment provides a foundation for the development of local collection management policies.
2. A number of libraries may use the data to compare/contrast collections in order to develop cooperative agreements for continued maintenance of existing strengths or cooperative acquisitions to enhance mutually spare collections. Cooperative retention, preservation, or last-copy retention policies might be based on the identification of existing strengths, as well.

The method of assessment chosen should be based on local conditions, demands, and expertise. Initially, only parts of the collection may be assessed—typically, the portion of the collection with the highest user demand. Methods include analyzing circulation data, interlibrary loan data, patron perception (client-centered analysis), or analyzing the size, depth, breadth, and growth of the existing collection (collection-centered analysis). In and of itself, an assessment has no meaning. Gathered data must be analyzed in light of known user needs and demands. It is through such evaluation of the collection *and* through the use of the collection that effective policy may be developed.

PEOPLE, CAN YOU FEEL IT? CHANGE IS EVERYWHERE...

Regardless of reasons cited, it appears that traditional thinking about collection management, in general, and interlibrary loan and acquisitions, in particular, must change. We would all be well-advised to develop a more holistic approach to all issues associated with the acquisition and dissemination of materials which our patrons have identified and requested.

It is apparent that given our limited resources, decisions regarding any aspect of such service cannot be made in isolation. Within this context, budgets proposed for acquisitions might take into account anticipated interlibrary loan and document delivery costs. Collection management and cooperative collection management policies might outline the types of materials that will be acquired solely on a temporary (interlibrary loan), or discrete (document delivery) basis. As traditional acquisitions activity decreases, human resources might be shifted to resource sharing activities. Or, to put it another way, resources might be shifted from traditional acquisitions to demand-based acquisitions.

Any of these activities might be addressed within a cooperative collection management policy or activity. A number of such ventures have been successfully launched, and those that have been the most successful share attributes which explicitly, or implicitly, incorporate the following beliefs:

1. The need for "core collections" and local development of collections is the first collection priority of any library.
2. Cooperative collection management is *an* answer, not *the* answer, to collection building problems.
3. Human interaction is a necessary component of cooperative collection management. Money and machines effectively enhance programs, but the foundation must be in a shared human

commitment and a recognition of the need to cooperate.
4. Cooperation exists on many levels—state, regional, and local—and therefore, varying levels of participation are both necessary and desirable.
5. The intent is to provide better, faster, and easier access to more information for the patrons of a group of libraries.
6. The cooperative is bound by a framework within which libraries can work, first and foremost, to achieve locally determined goals and objectives.

CALL TO ACTION

The fiscal environment we now find ourselves in makes it even more important to share the limited resources we have. Now, perhaps more than ever, we will have to cooperate with each other in order to deliver the services our users—our citizens—expect and deserve.

On a larger basis, each institution must recognize and act upon this resource-sharing imperative. The most effective environment in which to operate such a resource sharing collective is one in which each participating institution enters as an active partner dedicated to achieving mutually beneficial goals.

As with any proposed change in the status quo, there is a risk that discussions on this topic will center on semantics rather than substance or service (I refer to these as the "what-the-heck-is-CCM" arguments). Libraries are experiencing reduced abilities to collect, organize, and disseminate library materials. As library professionals search for solutions to these problems, it is important, if not imperative, that resource sharing efforts are developed and strengthened based on mutual needs. Concurrently, libraries must adopt a holistic approach to the management of collections in order to survive in an era of reduced budgets, increased publication, inflationary pricing for materials, and greater demand from users.

FEAR NOT...

These are exciting and challenging times for us as information professionals. Albeit, such times require a willingness to continually examine the worth of services provided in return for funds received. When speaking of change, we generally focus on what everyone else needs to do in order to make the situation better. Too rarely do we take a look at our own actions and think how we could change our behaviors to enhance service. I've heard a number of colleagues remark that it's easy to be cooperative when there's plenty of money, but the tight fiscal times to come will test our mettle as librarians who have traditionally expounded on the virtues of cooperation and reciprocity. In this practice, we are well-advised to heed Ghandi's admonition to "be the change."

Read—and think about—the articles which follow. The processes and projects described were developed by individuals and groups of dedicated librarians working hard to affect positive change. They have each been successful.

RLG And NCIP: A Brief Overview And Selected Bibliography

by Barbara McFadden Allen

The RLG (Research Libraries Group) conspectus was developed in 1980 by the Collection Management and Development Committee of the Research Libraries Group. The committee was comprised of one representative from each full and associate RLG member institution. David H. Stam served as Chairman of the committee and Paul Mosher served as Vice-Chairman. Anticipating the challenges of acquisitions budgeting in a period of inflationary pricing for library materials, the committee worked to identify a methodology in which RLG member libraries could better coordinate the growth and management of their collections. The result was the development of the RLG conspectus.

The conspectus, based on a set number of subject descriptors derived essentially from Library of Congress subject classifications, provided a consistent framework within which RLG member libraries could report subject intensity based on an agreed-upon number of descriptors.

In 1983, the Association of Research Libraries, working with RLG, began the North American Collections Inventory Project (NCIP). The project's long-term goal was to establish an online inventory of North America's research library collections for a variety of purposes. The basis for this inventory was the RLG conspectus.

Since the inception of the RLG conspectus and the NCIP, there have been a number of outstanding documents published detailing both the development and use of these tools. The reader is referred to these publications for a more thorough review of the subject.

Association of Research Libraries, Office of Management Studies. *Manual for the North American Inventory of Research Library Collections*, 1988 ed. Washington, D.C. The Association, 1988.

Dougherty, Richard M. "A Conceptual Framework for Organizing Resource Sharing and Shared Collection Development Programs." *The Journal of Academic Librarianship* 14 (November 1988): 287-91.

Farrell, David. "The NCIP: Option for Coordinated Collection Management." *Library Resources & Technical Services* 30 (January 1986):47-56.

Farrell, David and Jutta Reed-Scott. "The North American Collections Inventory project: Implications for the Future of Coordinated Management of Research Collections." *Library Resources & Technical Services* 33 (January, 1989):15-28.

Ferguson, Anthony W., Joan Grant, and Joel S. Rutstein. "The RLG Conspectus: Its Uses and Benefits." *College & Research Libraries* 49 (May, 1988):197-206.

Forcier, Peggy Cummings and Nancy N. Powell. "Collection Assessment in the Pacific Northwest: Building a Foundation for Cooperation." *Advances in Library Automation and Networking* 3 (1989):87-121. (Published by JAI Press).

Luquire, Wilson, ed. *Coordinating Cooperative Collection Development*. New York: Haworth Press, 1986. (This is a compilation of papers delivered in April, 1985 at "Coordinating Cooperative Collection Development: A National Perspective", a conference sponsored by the Illinois Board for Higher Education. An important work for the depth and breadth of coverage.)

Barbara McFadden Allen, issue co-editor, is Networking Consultant with the Illinois State Library, Springfield, Illinois.

MacEwan, Bonnie J. "The North American Inventory Project: A Tool for Selection, Education and Communication." *Library Acquisitions* 1 (1989): 45-50.

Millson-Martula, Christopher A. "The Greater Midwest Regional Medical Library Network and Coordinated Cooperative Collection Development: the RLG Conspectus and Beyond." *Illinois Libraries* 71 (January 1989): 31-9.

Mosher, Paul H. "Collaborative Collection Development in an Era of Financial Limitations." *Australian Academic and Research Libraries* 20 (March 1989):515.

Mosher, Paul H. "Collaborative Interdependence: the Human Dimensions of the Conspectus." *IFLA Journal* 16 (1990): 327-31.

Research Libraries Group. *North American Inventory Project: Means to an End; Minutes of the 109th meeting, October 22-23, 1986.* Washington, D.C. Association of Research Libraries, 1987.

Research Libraries Group. *RLG Collection Development Manual*, 2nd ed. Stanford, Calif.:Research Libraries Group, 1981.

Wood, Richard J. and Katina P. Strauch, eds. *Collection Assessment: A Look at the RLG Conspectus.* New York:Haworth Press, 1992. (This is a particularly thorough coverage of the subject, and includes an annotated bibliography by Jerry Seay, as well as a number of articles examining the applications, and limitations, of this methodology.)

The Krueger Method: An Introduction

by Georgine Olson

The Krueger Method, one of the first conspectus geared to use by smaller, non-automated libraries, is examined in the following three articles. Together, they show both the beginnings of the conspectus and the use to which it is being put nearly fifteen years later.

- First, Bill Erbes explains how and, more importantly, why the Krueger Method was originally conceived and developed by the Illinois Valley Library System.

- Second, Kim Bunner, then director of one of the original Krueger project libraries, explains how the different facets of the method were tested, evaluated, and changed by project libraries. She also reflects on the evolution of conspectus and what she feels is valuable in the Krueger Method, as well as the conspectus currently used most frequently in Illinois—the WLN-based Illinois Conspectus.

- Third, I present a quick overview of some of the more recent use of the Krueger Method, particularly focusing on client-centered analyses, in a variety of projects in Illinois, Colorado, Connecticut, and New Jersey libraries.

Illinois Valley Library System And The Development Of The Krueger Method

by Bill Erbes, adapted by Georgine Olson

The Illinois Valley Library System (IVLS) has long been committed to coordinated cooperative collection development as an efficient, effective resource sharing mechanism. IVLS is a multi-type, regional cooperative with 90 member libraries and headquarters located in Pekin, Illinois.

BEGINNINGS

The commitment to coordinated CCD began in 1977 when the IVLS Advisory Council recommended, and the system board concurred, that a moratorium be declared on expanding system funds for resource development in the headquarters library until system funding improved and an objective plan for resource development was established. One year later, a Blue Ribbon Committee was appointed to assist the system in developing such a plan.

In a memo to the system board on May 10, 1978, IVLS Executive Director Ray Howser stated, "It is urgent that we discover what library user needs are not being fulfilled by current library resources in IVLS; what resource strengths and weaknesses exist among our libraries; where unnecessary duplication of resources occurs; what subject areas need development within our system, and, finally, to design a plan, in concert with the ILLINET Cooperative Collection Development policies, which will encourage IVLS libraries to coordinate the development of resources." ILLINET is a resource–sharing cooperative whose members include all 2400 libraries in the Illinois regional library systems.

The Blue Ribbon Committee found it necessary to first evaluate the current information services provided by IVLS and to make recommendations prior to addressing total system resource development. The philosophy statement written by that committee says, in part, that "...a basic premise is that each library has an obligation to continually strive toward excellence in meeting the basic information and resource need of its clientele. The system's responsibility is to provide whatever is necessary to coordinate, supplement, and augment the local effort so that user needs are fulfilled in a time and place reasonably convenient for the user."

In its subsequent "Guidelines for Implementing High Quality Information Services," the Blue Ribbon Committee noted that, "Information services (i.e., reference, referral, and interlibrary loan) and coordinated collection development are interdependent and will be coordinated by the system as one service program." Furthermore, the committee believed that, "...quality service is of paramount importance and requires utilization of total resources of system libraries to fulfill requests in the most user beneficial and cost effective manner."

The IVLS board and membership agreed with those recommendations. An All-Library Meeting was held to explain the recommendations and to give librarians a chance to discuss the implications of the cooperative information services

Bill Erbes received his M.L.S. from the University of Illinois at Urbana-Champaign in 1981. Since mid-1993 he has been Internet Coordinator for Illinois Valley Library System, Pekin, Illinois. When the 1989 version of this article was written, he was Information Services Consultant for IVLS.

plan. In the meantime, the Blue Ribbon Committee made the decision to hire an outside consulting firm to help them with the difficult task of designing a cooperative collection development plan for IVLS.

KING RESEARCH PROJECT

In 1979, funding was received thorough the Illinois Interlibrary Cooperation Project. A proposal from King Research, Inc., then of Rockville, Maryland, was accepted, and by mid-1980 a contract was signed. Work on the project began in September 1980, with input from the Blue Ribbon Committee for its duration.

The King Research Project was divided into five tasks:

1. To address questions such as the ultimate purpose of cooperative collection development, the specific measurable objectives for a collection development plan, evaluation methodology, and the practical limitations of such a plan. These questions were to be addressed by King Research in concert with the Blue Ribbon Committee.
2. To create a description of existing collection development activities and to develop a means of determining collection strengths.
3. To formulate workable approaches to cooperative collection development and to delineate roles for individual libraries, system headquarters and resource libraries outside the system. The final outcome of the third task was to be the definition of several alternative approaches to cooperative collection development.
4. To develop procedures for comparing the selected alternatives.
5. To elaborate the implementation of the selected alternatives in terms of time schedules, financial plans, and responsibilities.

The King Research experiment considered four approaches to the gathering of data for collection assessment:

1. To identify subject strengths of individual libraries and groups of libraries.
2. To identify areas where subject demand exceeded available supply within the system.
3. To identify overlap of subject strengths in two or more libraries.
4. To display the results of those investigations so that planning for cooperative collection development could occur.

Furthermore, the collection assessment approaches were to be based on data collection that could be performed by clerical personnel.

The intent was to make the data collection as objective, comparable among libraries, and inexpensive as possible.

PRELIMINARY CONSIDERATION OF ASSESSMENT METHODS

The first of the four methods considered was library self-nomination of strengths—an approach already used in the *Directory of the Illinois Valley Library System*, IVLS's directory of member libraries. This approach has the advantage of being the least expensive way of identifying collection strengths and is a way of helping local staff become more aware of their own collections. Its disadvantages are that local staff may not be aware that their local collection represents a strength relative to other collections in the system, or they may consider a local collection area a strength while the system may contain a stronger collection elsewhere. Essentially, self-assessment has the flaw of lacking any standard for comparison among the member collections.

The second method involves expert review of library collections for strengths. With this approach, faculty from relevant university departments, practitioners in relevant fields, or libraries with subject specialties are used to assess collections in specific subject areas. This approach provides comparability among the visited collections and produces a consensus-based description of a collection's strengths. Those involved in assessing collections become aware of the resources available in the system and become expert in making referrals in their respective subject areas. The method is, however, costly. There is a limit to the number of collections a team can compare, and the approach may not be objective. That is, different teams may differ in their conclusions about essentially similar collections.

A third method is to check library holdings against standard lists or results of citation analysis. Though it has been used in school and public libraries, this approach has most often been used to assess academic library collections. The advantage of the procedure is the production of objective, comparable results for a set of libraries. Once the list has been determined, list checking is a relatively quick procedure that can be carried out by relatively untrained staff. If, in fact, a list can be designated as authoritative, this method gives an intelligible assessment of the collection's strength and provides a guide for future collection activities. It is the designation of an authoritative list that is the major difficulty with this method.

It is the fourth method, data collection and analysis of distribution of holdings compared with circulation and/or ILL requests, that was chosen for exploration in the King Research project. This approach involves taking a sample of books in the collection from either the shelflist or the stacks, and of books requested through interlibrary loan. The titles contained in each sample are examined in terms of subject, date of publication, or date of last circulation. Comparisons across samples allow examination of percentage of holdings in a given subject compared with percentageof books in circulation from the same subject class, or comparison of holdings with books requested through interlibrary loan. This method provides comparable data for those libraries studied. It allows local library staff to become more informed about their own collections as well as those of other members, and it allows data resulting from the study to be compared across time to assess the impact of changes in collection practice. Furthermore, the procedures for the data collection are well worked out and easy to specify.

DEVELOPMENT OF ASSESSMENT MANUALS

Upon receipt and analysis of the King Research report, IVLS was ready to proceed with the next phase of its long-range objective—the preparation of a step-by-step manual to be used by other systems and libraries. A Library Services and Construction Act (LSCA) Grant Proposal to underwrite the development of the manual was submitted to the Illinois State Library and funding was received. Entitled "Implementation of Coordinated/Cooperative Collection Development—A Planning Model for Systems," the proposal was intended to develop a process for cooperative collection development among all types of libraries. Emphasis was to be placed on the development of user-oriented acquisition policies at the local level and the determination of subject collection responsibilities at the system level. Statewide application of the process was also intended to help identify responsibilities of R&R (Reference and Research) Centers and other special resource centers. The basis for the entire process was to become the King Research methodology.

Essentially, it was felt that, even though the King Research report provided the instrument to assesscollection strengths, weaknesses, areas of unnecessary duplication among libraries, and unmet user needs within a system, a problem still existed in that there was no easy guide to follow in applying the King Research methodology. It seemed like the provision of such a guide would permit the implementation of coordinated cooperative collection development activities within

(and among) all types of libraries and library systems—and be adaptable to various levels of participation among member libraries. Such activities would then provide an objective means to assure that limited library materials budgets would be expended in more efficient and effective ways to meet more user needs. In so doing, libraries would enhance the expectations users and nonusers have for the information function of libraries.

Under the direction of Karen Krueger, a three-volume manual, *Coordinated Cooperative Collection Development for Illinois Libraries*, was produced.

The first volume is an overview manual. It explains cooperative collection development in general terms, describes benefits, reviews assessment methods used to date, and proposes a new approach for ILLINET. It describes the coordinated cooperative collection development approach that is the basis of the manual and provides a general overview intended to give library directors, staff, and governing authorities an understanding of the process and enough information to make a decision about their willingness and ability to participate in cooperative projects.

Volume two is a how-to manual for local libraries and describes, step-by-step, the procedures to be used in collecting data on holdings, use, and acquisitions. It lists the procedures for interpreting and using the data to guide local collection development decisions. It includes specific instructions, worksheets, forms, and numerous examples.

The third volume is a how-to manual for the regional library system. It describes, step-by-step, the procedures to be used in collecting and using data from system-mediated interlibrary loan, along with data from local libraries, to develop a coordinated cooperative collection development plan for the regional system. It includes specific instructions, worksheets, forms, examples, conversion tables, and information on data analysis.

NEXT STEPS

Though the Krueger manuals were an enormous accomplishment, it was felt by IVLS that still more needed to be done. Specifically, there was concern that the manuals were really models that had not been thoroughly tested by the kinds of libraries they were designed to guide. Therefore, a two-system (Illinois Valley Library System and Rolling Prairie Library System), two-year LSCA funded project was proposed. The goals of the project were: 1) for all types of libraries to begin to use the manual, 2) for libraries to modify the manual based on local need and use, and 3) for the experiences of those libraries to provide information in order to make necessary revisions to the manual. Six libraries from the Rolling Prairie Library System and seventeen libraries from the Illinois Valley Library System were involved in the test.

A significant outcome of the project was the development of an automated data analysis method using an IBM Personal Computer and LOTUS 1-2-3 software. It was felt the LOTUS 1-2-3 adaptation was necessary, as manual tabulation of data would be time-consuming, tedious, and prone to error. At the conclusion of the project, the software was made available to all Illinois library systems and to the Illinois State Library.

In January 1985, data analysis program manuals were published for Dewey Decimal classification schemes, Library of Congress classification schemes, and National Library of Medicine classification schemes.

In addition, the *Data Gathering Handbook for Collection Analysis* by Geri Schmidt was published. Its purpose was to serve as a supplement to the original Krueger manuals, and its methodology for data collection was compatible with the Krueger manual's. The data gathered through use of the Schmidt handbook could be tabulated using the same LOTUS program. However, the supplement was a simplified version of Krueger's manuals and omitted the philosophy and theory material that were included in Krueger's work.

All pertinent materials relating to the development of the Krueger Method that were produced by the Illinois Valley Library System are available through the system and the Illinois State Library. Libraries interested in a full investigation of the "Krueger Method" for coordinated cooperative collection development should examine the King Research, Inc. report, the Krueger manuals, the Schmidt supplements, and the LOTUS software. Also available is a 1984 external evaluation report of the first phase of the two-system coordinated cooperative collections development project.

NOTE: This article is an adapted and updated version of "If CCD is Good, CCCD is Better: the IVLS Approach", which first appeared in the January 1989 issue of Illinois Libraries and appears here with permission of the Illinois State Library.

The Krueger Manuals: A Case Study

by Kimberly Bunner

When asked to reflect upon being one of the original test sites for what has become known as the *Krueger Manuals*, I thought back to all the excitement we shared being a test site for what eventually formed a cornerstone of collection development history. [1] It is interesting to reflect upon the many changes in technology and theories that occurred over the past decade. Many elements in the *Krueger Manuals* were not only used in collection development, but were linked to library management by using output measurements and analyzing user satisfaction.

The Illinois Valley Library System (IVLS) is a multitype regional cooperative serving 90-member libraries in a ten county area surrounding Peoria, Illinois. It includes not only the major metropolitan area of Peoria, but many sparsely populated rural areas. Despite such diversity, these librarians share a unique willingness to cooperate with one another in the sharing of resources and ideas. In fact, in 1985 IVLS became the first multitype library system in Illinois. It seemed natural, even in 1982, that the "Krueger" project would include a variety of library types.

The group selected to test the methodology included a school library, an academic library, a large public library, and a small public library. A brief description of each participating library, as it was at that time, follows:

1. East Peoria Community High School serves the high school students of East Peoria, a city of approximately 19,000 separated from Peoria by the Illinois River.
2. Bradley University, founded in 1897 in Peoria, is privately endowed and offers graduate and undergraduate programs in business, liberal arts, and engineering.
3. Peoria Public serves a city of 127,000 with a manufacturing base rooted in heavy industry. The population of the metropolitan area is approximately 342,000.
4. Peoria Heights, a village of 7500, is completely surrounded by the city of Peoria. Given the reciprocal borrowing privileges afforded IVLS member libraries, many of the research needs of the community were met at the Peoria Public Library. In such an environment, the library needs of the Peoria Heights users were analogous to those of a branch library. However, one fourth of the users of Peoria Heights Public Library were Peoria residents.

At the time of the project, I was the Director of the Peoria Heights Public Library. Our total book collection was approximately 32,000 while the annual book budget was about $10,000. Our annual circulation was 59,000. We had neither an automated circulation nor an automated acquisition system. We did, however, have a dedicated staff of six who were enthusiastic about embarking on a project with Karen Krueger.

As a test site, we began by experimenting with and evaluating a variety of methods of collection-centered data gathering, all of which were ultimately rejected. Here are some of the methods we passed on:

Kimberly Bunner is the former Director of Peoria Heights Public Library. She received her B.A. from Illinois State University in 1978 and her M.L.S. from the University of Illinois at Urbana-Champaign in 1979. She is currently Manager, Reference and Technical Services, Parlin-Ingersoll Library, Canton, Illinois.

1. Self-nomination of subject strengths selected by individual libraries would not give a consistent, objective method for comparison.
2. The checking of standard lists did not work well for small public libraries that do not own enough of the titles on such lists to draw an adequate sample.
3. Using professors and research specialists to determine a core list of titles in specific areas did not seem to be economical or appropriate for the collection levels that would be found in the types of libraries expected to use the assessment tool we were developing.

We decided to use client-centered assessment, data gathering, and analysis. This data would form the methodology later delineated in the *Krueger Manuals*. Krueger's method focuses on the following five areas:

1. shelf list measurement,
2. random sampling and availability,
3. circulation and in-house use,
4. acquisitions, and
5. interlibrary loan.

What follows is a description of what happened at Peoria Heights Public Library during each of these steps. The *Krueger Manuals* describe the procedures and necessary formulas in detail. My remarks will be limited to our experiences in applying these processes.

THE PROCESS

We began with shelf list measurement. It was the first time the staff had experimented with statistical sampling. However, as a test site library we had the good fortune to embark on the project with the project coordinator, Karen Krueger, on site. Having Karen with us not only gave us constant encouragement but immediate answers to even the simplest of questions.

Our first step was to measure shelf list cards. There are many local cataloging practices that can create difficulty when using this method. In our specific case, the shelf list drawers had divider cards labeling Dewey call numbers that interfered with our measurements. Some of our catalog card stock was of noticeably different thickness. It was a challenge to find a measuring tool that included breakdowns to the ½₂" level—a level we felt we needed since some of our call number breakdowns were small. We also found it best to have the same person measuring the cards in order to assure the same strength was used in compressing the cards as well as in measuring them consistently. Our reference shelf list cards were filed separately from the other adult

nonfiction. Given the above inconsistencies coupled with the fact that many of the subject breakdowns in our collection were too small to properly measure, we opted to count cards as opposed to measuring them. This method proved far more workable for us.

Our second step was to determine the random sampling and availability of the collection. Here we used a team of two. One person counted cards and flagged selected cards. A second person then followed through and copied the call number and date of publication from the shelf list card and onto the data collection form. Our building logistics were such that much of this shelf list work could be done by circulation staff during slow periods. When that portion was completed, we checked the shelf for the availability of selected items.

The third step consisted of circulation and in-house use statistics. At the time of the study we used a manual Gaylord charging system and did not have the luxury of an automated circulation system. Since our book cards did not list publication dates, we felt the best method to complete this section was to note call numbers and publication dates as we checked out materials to patrons. Though this created a slight delay for our patrons, we found them generally understanding throughout the three weeks needed for us to obtain an adequate sample. While the ideal system would have been to include in-house use statistics in this portion, we had such little in-house activity that we could not serve as a reliable sample for that portion of the survey.

The fourth area of exploration was acquisitions. Unfortunately, Peoria Heights had lost one of its major tax revenue industries—Pabst Brewery, in 1981. Other industries, as well, had streamlined operations and moved services to other communities. The general economic climate in the entire area had declined, reflecting the change from an industry-based to a service-oriented society. In turn, the assessed valuation of many communities in the area declined dramatically. Tax supported institutions suffered drastic losses in revenue. At Peoria Heights Public Library, our acquisitions budget was reduced. Therefore, we did not have a large enough sample to participate in the acquisitions study, nor had records been kept in a manner that would have enabled us to reconstruct a sample from previous years.

The fifth area of collection development analysis was interlibrary loan. Within the region, our library system, IVLS, served as the interlibrary loan center for its members and, therefore, analyzed requests from all member libraries to determine regional subject deficiencies and strengths. However, many libraries did bypass

IVLS to do direct interlibrary loans using the OCLC subsystem. Gathering data for all ILL requests made by member libraries was more difficult than had been anticipated.

PRELIMINARY CONCLUSIONS

After completing the major portion of the data gathering, representatives of the test libraries met to determine what conclusions might be drawn from the information we now had and how this information could be used cooperatively. It was generally felt that the overall data upheld and reinforced many previously held assumptions. Although Peoria Public was much larger than Peoria Heights, our patron shared an interest in such "public library" areas such as home economics and the arts. Collection depth did, however, vary depending upon local budgetary resources. Peoria Public data revealed a heavier circulation in more technical categories such as economics/business, social problems, and engineering/technology. This supports the generally held assumption that they are a research hub for patrons of other public libraries in the area. While there were some similarities in subject area holdings between East Peoria Community High School and Peoria Heights Public Library, student research needs were reflected in East Peoria Community High School circulation, which showed an emphasis in social problems, psychology, and medicine. Bradley University data showed strengths in English literature, education, and business—all of which reflected their curriculum. With such a wealth of data, and some specific differences in user needs, we wondered how this data would be used to develop cooperative collection management agreements.

Analysis of availability and turnover rate were explored. Peoria Public had a lower availability rate than Peoria Heights. Did that mean that Peoria Public Library was not supplying enough copies of its works or did that mean the Peoria Heights Public Library had books sitting on the shelf not being used? We wondered if there was an easy answer to "What is an acceptable fill rate?" So, at Peoria Heights Public Library, we went one step further. We did a Materials Availability Survey to ascertain the patron's perceptions of met and unmet subject needs. Every patron entering the library received a survey form. During the test period we found the majority of our library use was for browsing purposes. We felt a longer survey period would be needed to make assumptions on subject fill rates. This was one of the first uses in our area incorporating the practices outlined in *Output Measures for Public Libraries*. [2]

RETOOLING THE PROCESS

One to two years after this first test, a supplement, *Data Gathering Handbook for Collection Analysis* by Geri Schmidt[3], was written to the *Krueger Manuals*. For the most part, this applied the Krueger methods to Lotus 1-2-3 software in order to facilitate data collection. This project included some members of the Rolling Prairie Library System as well as IVLS. At Peoria Heights we applied this software to our juvenile nonfiction collection. The software helped streamline data gathering. Again, there were no surprises in what we learned. Rather, we had confirmation and documentation of staff impressions about subject areas needing improvement.

TEN YEARS LATER: REFLECTIONS ON THE PROCESS AND ITS EVOLUTION

Collection management is growing and evolving. Different methods of assessment exist and decisions will have to be made in order to share that information. We still strive for data gathering methods that are quick and economical. The conclusions reached from assessment data depend upon the professional judgment of the librarian involved in the interpretation of the data. The persons responsible for selection in each area should be involved also. When one is the pioneer, people will find criticism of the original concept. The original concept is then modified and improved upon to create another methodology.

As I look back on the *Krueger Manuals*, I see many areas that were ahead of the times. In many ways these manuals were the first to experiment with applying collection management techniques to all types of libraries—not just the academics. Areas of future emphasis in the field of librarianship were emerging. The question of availability and its reflection on quality of service has become a standard output measure employed in many libraries today. To compare a library's acquisitions in a subject area to the circulation in that area could reveal some differences that might be of importance in allocating funds. While a library might not be totally demand driven, this information can be a valuable tool. Analyzing availability, circulation, and acquisitions can be an integral part of any library's long range planning and measuring of user satisfaction. The possibilities of analyzing interlibrary loan patterns by subject areas to determine collection deficiencies continues to be explored.

There were some criticism of these manuals. When first embarking on use of the three-volume *Krueger Manuals*, many libraries seemed overwhelmed. However, it is interesting to note that upon completion of the process, one of the criticisms was that the manuals did not have enough depth! As is so often the case with new ideas, once we experimented a little, we wanted more and more and more! We wanted to analyze more than our adult nonfiction collections; we now wanted to analyze juvenile collections, serial collections, and, somehow, apply these techniques to fiction collections.

A second criticism was noted by Geri Schmidt in her final report, *Report & Recommendations for Cooperative Collection Development Activities in the Illinois Valley Library System*.[4] The percentage of holdings or percentage of circulation did not give enough information when used to determine the extent of collections in other libraries. While the percentages were useful for internal evaluation, the use of numbers would put the information into better perspective for cooperative analysis.

A third criticism arose concerning uniformity within the state. While the methodology of the *Krueger Manuals* was developed as an easy, objective method to be used by a variety of library types, another project was emerging in Illinois. The Illinois Board of Higher Education had adopted a different set of standards and national codes based on the RLG Conspectus. These codes and methods of collection assessment were already being used in academic libraries in the state. The RLG Conspectus had a higher level breakdown for the larger libraries than had been developed in the *Krueger Manuals*. Since it was desirable to have one standard used for all libraries in Illinois, the State of Illinois chose this conspectus methodology. It would eventually incorporate the Pacific Northwest Conspectus and the WLN software to become known as the Illinois Conspectus.

There are concerns that arise about collection development that are not unique to the *Krueger Manuals*. One concern involves the usefulness of the data collected. While one might be disappointed in not finding something profound and unexpected, there is still value in the data. For internal management purposes, one can use the data to document areas of need to funding authorities. One can also determine the spending of limited resources and identify unused or outdated areas for weeding more intelligently.

The information weened from the analysis is useful in a cooperative environment, as well. Many libraries have formed cooperative groups. These can be defined by geography, library type, library size, special subject interests, or a combination of these factors. At the Parlin-Ingersoll Library, where I am currently employed, a coop-

erative arrangement has been made between our local high school, community college, and public library. We divided the subscriptions of some of the indexed, but lesser used, magazines among our three libraries. It has proven to be not only more economical, but has resulted in faster service for the customer because we fax requests for unowned titles to each other.

In the past decade, the advances in library automation have made data gathering easier. Many automated systems allow for collection breakdowns by call numbers. Not only can present holdings be broken down by call number, but acquisitions can be tracked by call number as well. Automation makes a variety of statistics available easily and can possibly eliminate the manual data gathering used in the *Krueger Manuals* a decade ago.

Availability is another area touched upon in the *Krueger Manuals* that obviously will reflect on patron satisfaction but also reinforces the need for continued evaluation. Analyzing what is not available will alert the selector to areas not found in the collection as well as previously unidentified areas that have been depleted due to lost, stolen, or unreturned items. Decisions will need to be made at the local level on acceptable availability and fill rates.

We continue to look at the median age of our collections. While this is a valuable indicator to us, it should be used with caution and in perspective. For example, if your medical collection includes a 1940 biography of the Mayo Brothers, the median age of the collection will be lowered. Likewise, if your medical collection has a 1940 book on cancer, your collection median age will be lowered. In the first case, your collection might have very up-to-date medical information with some historical titles. In the second case, your collection could be providing very serious misinformation. While some methods try to avoid this type of problem by using mean averages, the key point is that when examining age, each collection needs to be considered in context. The *Krueger Manuals* analyze the median age of the collection as a whole and the median age of those items in circulation. Again, used in the proper context, this information could be of value.

Presently, in Illinois, the State has endorsed the *Illinois Conspectus* and is currently working on building a statewide collection management database. Terry Weech succinctly describes the *Illinois Conspectus* method as being collection-centered; emphasizing both a qualitative examination of one's collection and a quantitative data gathering by shelf list measurement or title count.[5] From this data, a current level, acquisition level, and goal level of collection are developed. The data can then be fed into local, regional, and statewide computer databases along with other library statistical information. Libraries could compare their collections to others in the state by population, budget, and so on. Comprehensive subject areas in a collection would be identified and shared with everyone. The Illinois Conspectus approach attempts to include all items of a collection in particular subject areas. When considering a library's business management collection, the evaluator would consider books, videos, audio cassettes, magazines, reference sources, and online access to business information. It is all encompassing. Since the qualitative assessment could be biased by the evaluator, the quantitative data from the title counts puts these assessments into perspective. This combined effort will help make this data useful to the many types of libraries throughout Illinois.

Having worked with both methods, I feel most comfortable with a blending of the two. The *Illinois Conspectus* does attempt to emphasize a more holistic look at the collection. I feel one must view the access to a subject area regardless of the format. The qualitative overview coupled with the gathering of title counts puts the individual assessments into perspective. Naturally, a common ground must exist to share and compare data. The *Krueger Manuals* emphasis on circulation, acquisitions, interlibrary loan data, and availability is particularly useful as an internal monitoring of the collection. Automation has made data gathering much easier, but in a non-automated environment data collection can still be done by volunteer, clerical, or student help, which is a goal of the *Krueger Manuals*. After formally assessing a collection, determinations can be made on areas to improve internally and areas to explore for external development. Cooperative agreements do not have to be all encompassing, but simply mutually beneficial. These agreements will provide the groundwork of the future as libraries form partnerships and are linked together electronically.

References

1. Krueger, Karen. Coordinated Cooperative Collection Development for Illinois Libraries. 2d edition. Springfield, IL: Illinois State Library, 1983.
2. Zweizig, Douglas and Eleanor Jo Rodger. Output Measures for Public Libraries: A Manual of Standardized Procedures. Chicago: ALA, 1982.
3. Schmidt, Geri. Data Gathering Handbook for Collection Analysis. Springfield, IL: Illinois State Library, 1985.
4. Schmidt, Geri. Report & Recommendations for Cooperative Collection Development Activities in the Illinois Valley Library System. Oglesby, IL: Geri Schmidt, 1986.
5. Weech, Terry. CCM in Illinois: A Resource Book. 2d edition. Springfield, IL: Illinois Cooperative Collection Management Committee, 1992.

Krueger Lives: An Unscientific Exploration

by Georgine Olson

With the evolution of the WLN-based *Illinois Conspectus* over the last decade, it is not unusual for some of us Illinois librarians to consider that earlier Illinois product, *The Krueger Manual*, to be an antique relic of a long outmoded, once-exciting, cutting-edge Illinois experiment. However, there are libraries and library consortia in Illinois and around the country who are quite oblivious to the demise of the Krueger Method. They not only use it, but have evolved it and updated its processes and analysis software. Perhaps more significant is the encouraging frequency with which the client-centered analyses tools included in the *Krueger Manuals* are beginning to show up in new assessment projects of all kinds.

BLOOMINGTON-NORMAL COOPERATIVE REFERENCE SERVICES

In 1987, the Bloomington-Normal Reference Roundtable (Illinois) undertook the first of several Library Services and Construction Act (LSCA) funded projects to create a metropolitan area cooperative reference service operating between eleven multitype libraries. Their year-long analysis of reference services and collections leaned heavily on Krueger's methods of tracking patron use of collections, while using the subject areas of what is now the WLN Conspectus.

In succeeding years, the Roundtable produced a cooperative reference services handbook complete with mission statement and reference services policy, a reference collection union/acquisition list of over 3,400 titles, and an OCLC-based periodi-

cals union list of 13,000 titles. The reference core collection, periodical holdings, and, most recently, fledgling CD-ROM wide area network became the basis of several cooperative resource management projects. Each step has involved use studies of varying degrees of formality. It is quite probable that many current members of the Roundtable are unaware that the methods they use when considering new cooperative projects hark back to Krueger.

FICTION ASSESSMENT PROJECT

In 1991, when central Illinois' Corn Belt Library System and Lincoln Trail Libraries System embarked on their LSCA funded project to create a fiction assessment tool, again, Krueger methodologies came into play.

This project was unique in that it began with small public libraries. None of the ten participants served a community larger than 10,000 and most served 3,000 or less. For the most part, no one on the library staff had training in library science, much less an M.L.S. It was important that the assessment tool be easy to understand and the value of processes involved readily conceptualized ideas. Tracking patron use and demand, unmet needs and unvoiced expectations was as enlightening and valuable as sampling the collection for age, quality, and genre distribution.

Thanks to some State funding requirements, most public librarians in Illinois are familiar with various service evaluation strategies included in *Output Measures*, so they were not too taken aback with the somewhat revised reincarnations that Shay Baker, with the urging and blessing of

---

Georgine Olson, Issue Co-Editor, is Resource Sharing Consultant for Corn Belt Library System in Bloomington, Illinois.

CBLS and LTLS staff, wove into the fiction assessment procedures. It should not be forgotten that Karen Krueger, the author of the *Krueger Manuals*, was an important collaborator in the development of those very output measures.

New Jersey

Diane Macht Solomon reports that New Jersey's Northwest Regional Cooperative (Chester, NJ) performed a Krueger-based collection assessment in 1991. They used an earlier version of the Lotus spreadsheet software from Connecticut (see below) and revised analysis work forms so that there was one for shelflist information (Dewey and LC) and a master form for the Krueger age, circulation, acquisitions, and interlibrary loan studies. Of particular interest is the sheet developed by their CCD Committee with age guidelines for collection development based on the Krueger assessment categories and the CREW Method of collection weeding.

Mergers of regional library systems have put a temporary crimp in New Jersey's current major assessment efforts, but as recently as March 1993, the New Jersey Library Association and the New Jersey Association of Library Assistants co-sponsored a workshop on cost-effective collection development that included Krueger-based collection evaluation.

Colorado

At the Glenwood Springs-based Three Rivers Regional Library Service System Cooperative Collection Development Project, collection analysis is based on the Krueger model. Participants included 95 libraries consisting of public, school, and academic libraries. Data analysis components were modified versions of the Krueger originals and use dBASE software. Their three year cycle of activities began in 1990 with four main objectives:

1. To collect data on the adult and young-adult non-fiction collection and its use.
2. To produce reports for participating libraries—for both individual libraries and for the group as a whole.
3. To coordinate meetings for participants to discuss the reports produced and cooperative collection development activities.
4. To produce a written regional plan for cooperative collection development.

First, in 1990, both collection-centered and client-centered data was collected. Collection-centered data included:

1. shelf-list sampling to establish size and age of subject areas,
2. subject and retention analysis of periodical holdings, and
3. subject analysis of current acquisitions.

Client-centered data included:

1. subject analysis of circulation during representative sample periods, and
2. subject analysis of interlibrary loan requests.

Data was analyzed at either a first level of 20 subject areas or a second level of 121 subject areas. Each library received a subject analysis of its collection in all five data areas listed above. In addition, participants received two printed lists of periodical holdings: an individual library list and a group union list.

In 1991, the project used the 1990 data to aid in qualitative analysis of individual collections. Libraries were to identify subject strengths and indicate a level of acquisition commitment in those areas. A combined list of subject strengths of participants was to be produced. Discussion of cooperative collection development activities was to continue.

In 1992, a regional plan for cooperative collection development was to be written.

Connecticut

Out of the Southwestern Connecticut Library Council in Bridgeport, Connecticut comes this quote from the 1992 introduction to their instructions for the use of *Coordinated/Cooperative Collection Assessment—Version 2.0*.

In 1983, the Illinois Library and Information Network sought to provide "a methodology for data collection and a process for interpreting and using the data in developing coordinated cooperative collection development plans." To this end, they produced a series of Lotus based programs for analyzing collection data that were founded in part on the principles espoused in Douglas L. Zweizig's *Test of Data Collection Approaches to Coordinated/Cooperative Collection Development*. The programs, written by Karen Bills, have since been used in a number of state and regional collection assessment projects around the country. over the years, the programs have become dated—especially with the advent of DDC20.

In 1987/1988, the libraries of Southwestern Connecticut used what has since become known as the 'Krueger Method' to guide them in revamping their collection development policies and in the exploration of a plan for cooperative purchasing. Since the original project was completed, some libraries sought to reevaluate their collections and others wanted to participate in a new round of analysis. With the original programs being dated, the Southwestern Connecticut Library Council contracted with Diane Pikul and Paul Simon for revisions. Permission to update these programs was granted by the original author, Ms. Karen Bills.

The Master Programs for the Collection Assessment Project have now been revised to evaluate materials published through 1994 and are designed to run on an IBM PC with a hard disk drive and wide-carriage printer. All programs operate on macros created within Lotus 1-2-3 (version 2.01) and now function via a menu screen. Usage requires only a minimal knowledge of Lotus 1-2-3.

It would appear that, like most good tools (in librarianship and otherwise), what we know as the *Krueger Method* is alive, well, and continually evolving.

WLN Conspectus: An Introduction

by Georgine Olson, Issue Co-Editor

The WLN Conspectus is examined in three articles that, together, give an explanation of the conspectus and an examination of how it has been used in two different venues.

- First, WLN's Sally Loken presents a basic introduction to the Conspectus, its arrangement, and continuing evolution as a collection management tool.

- Second, Nancy Powell explains how the WLN Conspectus was put to use as a collection management tool in a small, essentially non-automated academic library.

- Third, June Pinnell-Stephens writes about the role of the WLN Conspectus in cooperative collection development and management in Alaska libraries.

The WLN Conspectus

by Sally Loken

Conspectus can mean, in some instances, either a survey, overview, or outline of the subjects in a collection. However, conspectus is also a method—the method of using the outline as the structure for systematic assessment of a library collection. Libraries use both the outline and the method to describe their collections and collection goals, using common definitions.

The WLN Conspectus was adapted from the RLG Conspectus to support cooperative collection development among libraries in the Pacific Northwest. It is now in use in hundreds of libraries across North America, as well as Australia and New Zealand. Individual libraries use it as a tool for internal collection management and for communicating the strengths and weaknesses of their collections to their users, funding sources, and supporters. Groups of libraries use the WLN Conspectus to support cooperative collection development activities, and there are several statewide CCM programs that rely on the WLN Conspectus structure and methodology.

The WLN Conspectus was formerly the Pacific Northwest Conspectus. In 1990, WLN became the new home of conspectus services that had been developed and provided by the Pacific Northwest Collection Development (PNCD) Program and its predecessor: the Library and Information Resources for the Northwest (LIRN) Program. PNCD staff built on the experience of Alaska librarians to design a modification of the RLG Conspectus that could be used to describe the collections of all types and sizes of libraries. The LIRN and PNCD programs provided the tools and training that 225 libraries used to assess their collections and create a regional collection assessments database. Tom Dorst, the program's evaluator, called this the single most successful cooperative collection development project of the 1980s.

To accomplish their goals for adapting the RLG Conspectus, PNCD staff provided an abridged reporting level for describing smaller collections, subdivided the six RLG collection-level indicators (0 through 5) into a total of ten levels to provide greater specificity at the 1- 2- and 3-levels, and provided a conspectus framework for Dewey as well as the LC classification system.

STRUCTURE OF THE WLN CONSPECTUS

The WLN Conspectus is explicitly hierarchical, containing 24 broad subject divisions:

- Agriculture
- Anthropology
- Art & Architecture
- Biological Sciences
- Business & Economics
- Chemistry
- Computer Science
- Education
- Engineering & Technology
- Geography & Earth Sciences
- History & Auxiliary Sciences
- Language, Linguistics & Literature

Sally Loken graduated from the University of Washington in 1971. She received her M.L.S. from U.W. in 1974 and her M.P.A. from Evergreen State College in 1982. Between 1978 and 1991, she served as Assistant Director for Central Services at Timberland Regional Library System headquartered in Olympia, Washington. Since 1991, she has been Coordinator of Collection Assessment Services for WLN, Lacey, Washington.

- Law
- Library Science, Reference & Generalities
- Mathematics
- Medicine
- Music
- Performing Arts
- Philosophy & Religion
- Physical Education & Recreation
- Physical Science
- Political Science
- Psychology
- Sociology

Each division is subdivided into categories, which represent the second tier of the hierarchy, and the categories are further subdivided into subject descriptors. Within each of the two sets of 24 divisions there are approximately 500 categories and more than 4000 subjects. The WLN Conspectus for the LC classification system has a total of 4805 lines; the Dewey version has 4714. Libraries use the structure as is appropriate to their collections. For smaller libraries, the category level is often the most useful for describing the collection. Special libraries use the subject level for areas that are collected in depth, and the division and category levels for other areas, as needed. For each of the 24 divisions, worksheets are available at both the abridged category level and the more detailed subject level.

The number of category and subject lines in a division depends generally on how the LC and Dewey classification schemes treat the subjects that are included in the division. For example, in the LC ART & ARCHITECTURE division there are 11 categories and 264 subject lines. In the Dewey treatment of this division there are ten categories and 356 subject lines. Collection assessment results for LC and Dewey libraries can be directly compared at the division level only. To meet the needs of libraries working on group assessment projects that include both Dewey and LC libraries, the PNCD staff developed correspondence tables for LC and Dewey conspectus lines at the category level.

THE CONSPECTUS METHOD

In the *WLN COLLECTION ASSESSMENT MANUAL, 4TH EDITION*, Mary Bushing and Nancy Powell describe the conspectus method as being "...an organized process for systematically analyzing and describing a library collection using standardized definitions." Their 1992 manual updates the 3rd edition of the *Pacific Northwest Collection Development Manual* and is the basic resource for collection assessment using the WLN Conspectus. The steps in conspectus methodology are as follows:

1. Plan and prepare for the assessment. In addition to determining the goals, scope, organization, and management of the project, this step may include the preparation or updating of the library's collection development policy.
2. Examine the collection subject by subject. Include all cataloged and uncataloged materials, electronic formats, media, realia, serials, documents, archival collections, etc., that are currently available to library users. Make good use of the information you already have about the collection and select from standard collection assessment techniques as appropriate.
3. Record the data gathered, using concise comments that describe significant characteristics of the depth and breadth of each subject area, including the number of titles in each format. Note approval plans, cooperative agreements, preservation policies, and similar factors that effect collection building.
4. Analyze the data collected to determine collection and acquisition level.
5. Assign to each subject numeric ratings for the collection level and acquisition commitment.
6. Determine and assign to each subject a numeric rating for the collection goal.
7. Assign a language code for those areas other than English.
8. Record the ratings and the comments on the conspectus worksheets.
9. Use the reports to describe collection strengths and weaknesses and make collection management decisions.
10. Enter the information into the library's collection assessment database.

RATING THE COLLECTION

Standardized numerical ratings are used to describe the current collection level, the acquisition commitment, and the goal level for the collection.

- **Current Collection (CL)** is a measure of the strength of the collection compared to the universe of available materials.
- **Acquisition Commitment (AC)** reflects the current growth of the collection.
- **Collection Goal (GL)** is based on the library's mission, programs and user needs. It communicates the library's target level for the collection.
- **Preservation Commitment (PC)** is optional. Libraries may record this for a subject area, using a locally agreed-upon definition, since nationally accepted codes and definitions have not yet been established to record preservation and conservation information.

The numeric ratings for reporting CL, AC, and GL are on a ten-point scale or continuum, from 0 to 5. Definitions excerpted from the *Manual* follow:

- 0   The Library does not collect in this subject
- 1a Minimal level, uneven coverage
- 1b Minimal level, even coverage
- 2a Basic information level, introductory
- 2b Basic information level, advanced
- 3a Basic study or instructional support level
- 3b Intermediate study or instructional support level
- 3c Advanced study or instructional support level
- 4   Research level
- 5   Comprehensive level

Language codes include:

- E   English language material predominates; little or no foreign language material in the collection.
- F   Selected foreign language material included, in addition to the English language material.
- W   Wide selection of foreign language material in all applicable languages.
- Y   Material is primarily in one foreign language. (The comments field should indicate the specific language.)

Automated Support for Collection Assessment

WLN provides several analyses to support the collection assessment process. The WLN Collection Analysis Report is a statistical analysis of the collections of one or more libraries. Designed to replace laborious shelflist counting, it calculates totals and percentages within Conspectus categories and subject descriptors. Results can be organized by publication date ranges, languages, intellectual level, or any element of the MARC record.

WLN's title overlap analyses provide a statistical summary of unique and multiply held titles by Conspectus lines, with optional title lists. And the WLN automated comparison of a library's holdings with the file of *Books for College Libraries*, 3rd Edition (BCL3), provides a statistical summary of matching and non-matching BCL3 records by Conspectus line, as well as title lists in Conspectus order. A similar technique is used to produce a gap analysis when the joint collection of a group of libraries is compared with a target collection.

Software Flexibility and Support for Local Needs

In collaboration with Conspectus users, WLN has expanded and enhanced the PC software that was developed by PNCD to create and maintain a database of collection assessments. New searching and reporting capabilities have increased the usefulness of data stored in the original three files (the Conspectus, Library and Assessment Files, plus any interdisciplinary files the user creates). Additionally, at the request of users, a complete module for Collection Management Information has been added. This allows libraries to organize by Conspectus lines data such as circulation, interlibrary lending and borrowing, acquisitions, budgets, collection growth, weeding, selection responsibilities, and other critical pieces of collection management information. Also, the WLN Collection Analysis Report can be uploaded to create a Collection Analysis File in the software package.

The latest release, *WLN Conspectus Software Version 5.0*, supports not only the local addition of Conspectus category and subject lines to meet institutional, regional, and international needs, but also the addition of entirely new divisions. For example, the fiction assessment structure (developed, with LSCA funding, by the Corn Belt Library System and the Lincoln Trail Libraries System in Illinois) is now available on diskette for uploading into the Conspectus File in the software. Software users can print worksheets for the fiction divisions, as well as the basic 24 divisions, as needed. In addition, the New York Metropolitan Reference and Research Library Agency (METRO) has made its Metro Music Division available to WLN Conspectus users. This structure for assessing music collections is organized differently and offers more subject specificity than other "authorized" conspectus music divisions and is a useful tool for all libraries with large music collections.

A group of hospital librarians in Washington State has begun the development of an alternative Medicine division that will follow the NLM classification system with corresponding LC call numbers provided. This scheme will provide more subject detail than the "authorized" LC Medicine division, which provides LC call numbers with NLM correspondences. This option for describing medical collections will be available to WLN Conspectus Software users in 1994.

USES OF CONSPECTUS INFORMATION

The Conspectus is a collection management tool for individual libraries and for groups of libraries that are working collaboratively on cooperative collection development. Its benefits and uses have been described extensively in library literature, focusing on the rational, objective basis that collection assessment provides for accountability in budgeting and priority setting for collection growth; the value of conspectus reports as tools for communicating the shape and needs of the collection to its user community, funding sources, accrediting agencies, and resource-sharing partners; and the enhanced skills in collection development that library staff acquire as they learn and use the process. As Conspectus usersgain experience, nationally and internationally, they are developing creative applications of the concept and are requesting more sophisticated automated support. WLN is pleased to be the provider of the WLN Conspectus and to work in partnership with its users to develop and improve the tools of collection management.

References

Sharon L. Baker, *Fiction Collection Assessment Manual.* Patricia J. Boze, ed. Champaign, IL: Lincoln Trail Libraries System, 1992.

Mary Bushing and Nancy Powell. *WLN Collection Assessment Manual.* 4th ed. Lacey, WA: WLN, 1992.

Mary Bushing, "The Conspectus: Possible Process and Useful Product for the Ordinary Library," in *Collection Assessment: A Look at the RLG Conspectus,* ed. by Katina Strauch and Richard J. Wood (New York: Haworth Press, 1992), 81-95.

Tom Dorst, "Pacific NW Conspectus Database Program Evaluation for the Period May 1987 to June 1989," *Pacific Northwest Collection Assessment & Development Newsletter* No. 22 (July 1989), 1-2.

Peggy Forcier, "Building Collections Together: The Pacific Northwest Conspectus," *Library Journal* 113:7 (April 15, 1988): 35-40.

Joan Grant, "The Conspectus: An Important Component of a Comprehensive Collection Management Program," in *Collection Assessment: A Look at the RLG Conspectus,* ed. by Katina Strauch and Richard J. Wood (New York: Haworth Press, 1992), 97-103.

Guide for Written Collection Policy Statements. 2nd ed. American Library Association. Subcommittee on Guidelines for Collection Development. Chicago: ALA, 1989.

June Pinnell-Stephens, "A Management Information System Using the WLN Conspectus Software," *WLN Participant,* v.11 no. 6 (Nov./Dec. 1992): 12-14.

June Pinnell-Stephens, "The WLN Conspectus in Alaska," *WLN Participant* (Nov./Dec. 1991): 6-8.

Dennis Stephens, "Multi-Type Library Collection Planning in Alaska: A Conspectus-Based Approach," in *Collection Assessment: A Look at the RLG Conspectus,* ed. by Katina Strauch and Richard J. Wood (New York: Haworth Press, 1992), 137-149.

Kent Underwood, "Developing Supplemental Guidelines for Music: A Case Report," in *Collection Assessment: A Look at the RLG Conspectus,* ed. by Katina Strauch and Richard J. Wood (New York: Haworth Press, 1992), 157-168.

Weech, Terry. *CCM in Illinois: A Resource Book.* 2nd ed. Springfield: Illinois Cooperative Collection Management Coordinating Committee, 1992.

CONSPECTUS DATABASE WORKSHEET - LC

Division: ART AND ARCHITECTURE

Library: _____
Date: _____
By: _____

LC CLASS	LINE NUMBER	DIVISION, CATEGORIES and SUBJECTS	COLLECTION & LANGUAGE CODES				COMMENTS
			CL	AC	GL	PC	
	ART000	ART AND ARCHITECTURE					
AM	ART001	Museums, Collectors & Collecting					
AM-9	ART002	General Works					
AM10-100	ART003	Description & History of Museums by Country					
AM101	ART004	Description & History of Individual Museums					
AM111-160	ART005	Museology, Museum Methods, Techniques, etc.					
AM200-237	ART006	Collectors & Collecting, Private Cabinets, etc.					
AM301-396	ART007	Collectors & Collecting, by Region or Country					
AM401	ART008	Individual Heterogeneous Collections					
CJ1-6661	ART008.5	Numismatics					
CJ4810-5450	ART008.51	Tokens					
CJ5501-6661	ART008.52	Medals & Medallions					
N1-9211	ART009	Visual Arts in General					
N61-72	ART009.5	Theory, Philosophy, Ethics					
N81-390	ART010	Study & Teaching					
N400-5098	ART011	Special Museums, Galleries, etc.					
N510-880	ART012	Special Museums, Galleries - United States					
N908-910	ART013	Special Museums, Galleries - Other American Cities					

Copyright 1986 Pacific NW Conspectus Database/Adapted from RLG Conspectus Worksheet

CONSPECTUS DATABASE WORKSHEET – Dewey

Library: _____
Date: _____   By: _____

Division: ART AND ARCHITECTURE

Dewey CLASS	LINE NUMBER	DIVISION and CATEGORIES	COLLECTION & LANGUAGE CODES				COMMENTS
			CL	AC	GL	PC	
	ARD000	ART AND ARCHITECTURE					
069	ARD005	Museology (Museum Science)					
700	ARD010	The Arts, Fine & Decorative Arts (20th: formerly also 704.92; 18th: 708 Collections only; 16th: 704 Essays & lectures only)					
710	ARD020	Civic & Landscape Art					
720	ARD030	Architecture					
730 (20th:also 731.2/.3/.4/.5)	ARD040	Plastic Arts - Sculpture (20th: formerly 732.3-.9 Comp. works on Oriental sculpt. before ca. 500, 732.4 Comp. works on Buddhist, Jain, Hindu sculpt., 731.1)					
740	ARD050	Drawing & Decorative Arts					
750	ARD060	Painting & Paintings (20th: formerly 751.72)					
760	ARD070	Graphic Arts, Printmaking & Prints					
770	ARD080	Photography & Photographs					

Collection Assessment for Anchorage Municipal Libraries - Anchorage, AK

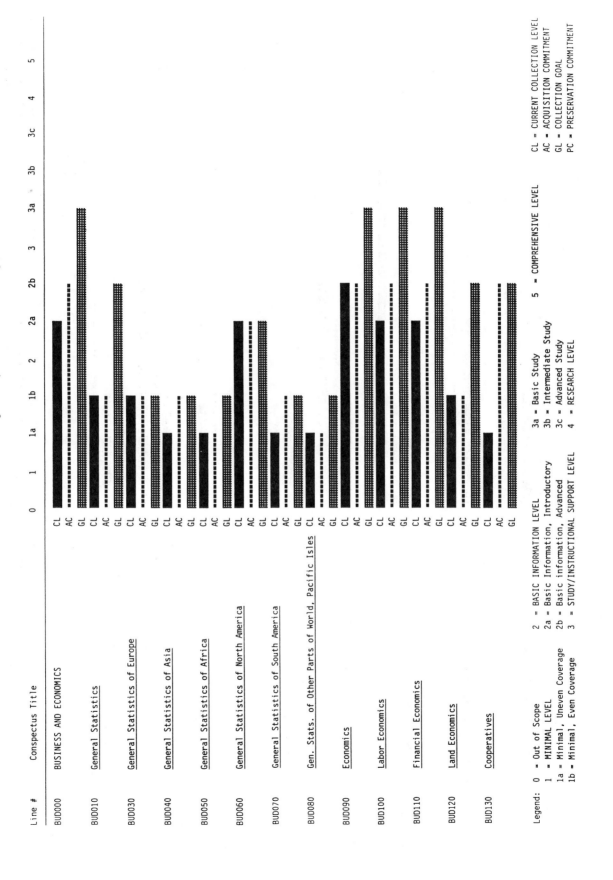

Division Report for Anchorage Municipal Libraries - Anchorage, AK

DIVISION — scale: 0 1 1a 1b 2 2a 2b 3 3a 3b 3c 4 5

Divisions (each with CL = Current Collection Level, AC = Acquisition Commitment, GL = Collection Goal):

- PHYSICAL EDUCATION AND RECREATION
- ENGINEERING AND TECHNOLOGY
- GEOGRAPHY AND EARTH SCIENCES
- LANGUAGE, LINGUISTICS, AND LITERATURE
- MATHEMATICS
- PHILOSOPHY AND RELIGION
- POLITICAL SCIENCE
- PSYCHOLOGY

Legend:
0 = Out of Scope
1 = MINIMAL LEVEL
1a = Minimal, Uneven Coverage
1b = Minimal, Even Coverage

2 = BASIC INFORMATION LEVEL
2a = Basic Information, Introductory
2b = Basic Information, Advanced
3 = STUDY/INSTRUCTIONAL SUPPORT LEVEL

3a = Basic Study
3b = Intermediate Study
3c = Advanced Study
4 = RESEARCH LEVEL

5 = COMPREHENSIVE LEVEL

CL = CURRENT COLLECTION LEVEL
AC = ACQUISITION COMMITMENT
GL = COLLECTION GOAL
PC = PRESERVATION COMMITMENT

Collection Assessment for University of Alaska - Fairbanks - Fairbanks, AK

Line #	Conspectus Title		0	1	1a	1b	2	2a	2b	3	3a	3b	3c	4	5
GE0106	Regional Geology - Australasia	CL													
		AC													
		GL													
GE0107	Regional Geology - Arctic Regions	CL													
		AC													
		GL													
GE0108	Regional Geology - Antarctic Regions	CL													
		AC													
		GL													
GE0109	Mineralogy	CL													
		AC													
		GL													
GE0110	Petrology (General)	CL													
		AC													
		GL													
GE0111	Igneous Petrology	CL													
		AC													
		GL													
GE0112	Sedimentary Petrology	CL													
		AC													
		GL													
GE0113	Metamorphic Petrology	CL													
		AC													
		GL													
GE0114	Dynamic & Structural Geology (General)	CL													
		AC													
		GL													
GE0115	Geochemistry	CL													
		AC													
		GL													
GE0116	Volcanoes	CL													
		AC													
		GL													
GE0117	Seismology	CL													
		AC													
		GL													
GE0118	Coral Reefs	CL													
		AC													
		GL													

Legend:
0	= Out of Scope	2	= BASIC INFORMATION LEVEL	3a	= Basic Study	5	= COMPREHENSIVE LEVEL
1	= MINIMAL LEVEL	2a	= Basic Information, Introductory	3b	= Intermediate Study		
1a	= Minimal, Uneven Coverage	2b	= Basic Information, Advanced	3c	= Advanced Study		
1b	= Minimal, Even Coverage	3	= STUDY/INSTRUCTIONAL SUPPORT LEVEL	4	= RESEARCH LEVEL		

CL = CURRENT COLLECTION LEVEL
AC = ACQUISITION COMMITMENT
GL = COLLECTION GOAL

39

Division Report for Montana State University - Bozeman, MT

DIVISION	CL	AC	GL	COMMENTS
AGRICULTURE	3cE	3cE		
ANTHROPOLOGY	1bE	1aE	2bE	2151 volumes. Weak, uneven, older materials.
ART AND ARCHITECTURE	2aE	2aE	3aE	Some document support.
CHEMISTRY	3aE	2bE	3cE	Good journal support, strong documents, indexing non-english serials
COMPUTER SCIENCE	2aE	1bE	3cE	2327 volumes. 54% of BOOKS FOR COLLEGE LIBRARIES; Strong journal support.
BUSINESS AND ECONOMICS				18,000+ titles. Good Journal & Doc support, including CD-ROM info.
GEOGRAPHY AND EARTH SCIENCES	3cE	3bE		
HISTORY AND AUXILIARY SCIENCES	2aE	1aE	3aE	19,417 volumes. Strength in European, Eastern Asian & U.S. 67 journals.
LAW	1aE	1aE	1bE	Supported by U.S., U.N., Canadian and Montana documents. 3a for Montana documents.
MATHEMATICS	3bE	2bE	3cE	6176 titles, Engineering & Education support. Major serials (420+ titles) with long runs. Monographs current (30 yrs). Computer Science Support.
MUSIC	1bE	1aE	2bE	8216 volumes plus departmental collections; 49% books for college library.
PHILOSOPHY AND RELIGION	1aE	1bE	2aE	minimal coverage of most subjects, minor strength in logic.
PERFORMING ARTS	1bE	1aE	2bE	2300+ titles, mainly Motion Pictures & Theater. Strong literature support at 2b level. Older Monographs.
PHYSICAL EDUCATION AND RECREATION	1bE	1aE	2bE	Emphasis on conditioning, education, college athletics. Also support by Docs, journals, & Nutrition material.
PHYSICAL SCIENCES	3aE	1bE	3cE	heavily supported with government documents & journals.
POLITICAL SCIENCE	1bE	1aE	2bE	Supplemented by U.S., Canadian & International Docs. Eurocentric & Amerocentric, supported by strong history. Major indexes but not strong serials.
PSYCHOLOGY	2aE	1aE	2bE	Little clinical material because of program emphasis.
SOCIOLOGY	2aE	1bE	2bE	10,500+ titles. Strong journal, general Ref & Doc support. Older monographs, undergraduate emphasis.
ENGINEERING AND TECHNOLOGY	2aE	1bE	3aE	In all but mining engineering topics, strongly supported with documents.

Legend:
0 = Out of Scope
1 = MINIMAL LEVEL
1a = Minimal, Uneven Coverage
1b = Minimal, Even Coverage
2 = BASIC INFORMATION LEVEL
2a = Basic Information, Introductory
2b = Basic information, Advanced
3 = STUDY/INSTRUCTIONAL SUPPORT LEVEL
3a = Basic Study
3b = Intermediate Study
3c = Advanced Study
4 = RESEARCH LEVEL
5 = COMPREHENSIVE LEVEL

CL = CURRENT COLLECTION LEVEL
AC = ACQUISITION COMMITMENT
GL = COLLECTION GOAL
PC = PRESERVATION COMMITMENT

Division Comparison – Selected Libraries With Fewer Than 20,000 Volumes

HISTORY AND AUXILIARY SCIENCES

NUC	LIBRARY	CL	AC	GL	COMMENTS
MBAr	Sturgis Library	2aE	2aE	2aE	9663 t; med age: General Coll.: 1980; Historical Coll.: 1881; [cc: 568 t; med age: 1964; Shipping Merchants, Sea Captains, comprehensive Cape Cod early history 1640-present, genealogies of Cape Cod families, Indian histories, Barnstable Church records, cemetary inscriptions of Cape Cemetaries]
MBArL	Barnstable Law Library	0	0	0	
MBOu	Jonathan Bourne Public Library	1aE	1aE	1bE	1978 circ t; 147 ref; 243 large print; med age: 1975; Bourne Town Reports: 1884-1989; 5 videos; 4 magzines, National Geographic: 1914-1945, 1948-present, Yankee 1959-60, 1962-present; Newspapers on microfilm: Bourne Courier 1984-1989; Bourne Enterprise 1985-1989; Bourne Pioneer 5/16/1890-12/31/1899; [cc: 140 t; med age: 1965]
MBRe	Brewster Ladies Library	1aE	1aE	1bE	1902 t; med age: 1962; 23 VT, 0 journals; 1014 biography not assigned to subject classification; [cc: 216 t; med age: 1968]; even coverage of European and Asian travel, good Eastern United States travel info
MBReC	Cape Cod Museum of Natural History	1aE	1aE	1aE	196 t; med age: 1973; emphasis on natural history travel, description, naturalist biography, and archaeology; [cc: 32 t; med age; 1968; archeology]
MCEn	Centerville Public Library	1bE	1bE	2aE	2589 t; med age: 1975; many excellent titles and well-used; [cc: 40 t; med age: 1970; 974, 69 t; med age: 1970]
MCHa	Eldredge Public Library	1bE	1bE	1bE	3021 t; med age: 1978; 1 magazine; 52 videos; 40% plc; genealogy reference collection 1870 t; Gen. Coll., 6 periodicals w/indexes; 24" of manuscript, 3000 volumes in total; [cc: 178 t]
MCOt	Cotuit Library	1bE	1bE	1bE	2290 t; med age: 1968; reference, juvenile & YA support; 3 periodicals; [cc: 129 t; med age: 1964]; biographies
MEA	Eastham Public Library	1bE			3500 t; med age: 1983; [cc: 500 t; from 900-999; med age: 1930]
MFAl	Falmouth Public Library	1bE	1aE	1bE	7737 t; med age: 1977; 19 periodicals; InfoTrac, National Newspaper Index; complete microfilm; NYT + Index; Boston Globe 1980-83,86-present; basic coverage with emphasis on US History and Cape Cod history; significant well selected individual biography collection; significant Massachusetts and Cape Cod genealogical sources; [cc: 191 t; med age: 1950; complete microfilm Falmouth Enterprise 1896--; complete microfilm Cape Cod Times 10/19/36-, 1 reel microfilm Cape Cod Independant various dates from 12/2/1892-9/1920, 8 reels microfilm Genealogical notes of Cape Cod families, 2 reels microfilm (Cape Cod) US Census of 1850, 8 reels microfilm Town of Falmouth Records 1661-1878, 46 fiche Mass. Vital Records of Falmouth 1668-1892, 1 microfilm reel List of burials in Woods Hole 1788-1968]
MGKj	Morton Grove Public Library--Childr	2aE	1bE	2aE	900s consist of about 41 shelves of books (about 2,500) books); many are worn and dated, World War II books in particular. Many new titles on third-world countries, etc. Heavy weeding needed based on circulation, age, and condition of book.
MHAr	Brooks Free Library	1bE	1bE	1bE	3280 t; 19 ref; med age: 1965; 15 journals including Cape Cod Life -1990; 1 Civil War Video; 11 audio tapes; VF: Topic headings, broad Civil War Collection; Genealogy and non-circulation; [CC: valuable Cape Cod Collection includes books, maps, pamphlets, diaries & old magazines; unique & historical; Harwich Independent Newspaper (late 1800's-1940's on microfilm); strong genealogy collection 1500 plus titles; pc of 5 is for Hawich History only]; Children's dept, 342 t plus reference; biographies 220 t;

Legend:

0 = Out of Scope	2 = BASIC INFORMATION LEVEL	3a = Basic Study	5 = COMPREHENSIVE LEVEL
1 = MINIMAL LEVEL	2a = Basic Information, Introductory	3b = Intermediate Study	
1a = Minimal, Uneven Coverage	2b = Basic information, Advanced	3c = Advanced Study	
1b = Minimal, Even Coverage	3 = STUDY/INSTRUCTIONAL SUPPORT LEVEL	4 = RESEARCH LEVEL	

CL = CURRENT COLLECTION LEVEL
AC = ACQUISITION COMMITMENT
GL = COLLECTION GOAL
PC = PRESERVATION COMMITMENT

WLN Automated Collection Analysis for XXX University Library

LV/Line #	Call # Range / Title	pre-1900	1900-1919	1920-1939	1940-1949	1950-1954	1955-1959	1960-1964	1965-1969	1970-1974	1975-1979	1980-1984	1985-1989	1990-	totals
D / EC0000	BUSINESS AND ECONOMICS	242 5.4^ 0.7>	246 4.3^ 0.7>	653 5.6^ 2.0>	649 6.5^ 1.9>	700 6.5^ 2.1>	1120 7.1^ 3.4>	2013 7.2^ 6.0>	5234 8.3^ 15.7>	7237 9.2^ 21.7>	5350 9.6^ 16.1>	6426 10.8^ 19.3>	3117 9.8^ 9.4>	333 10.9^ 1.0>	33320 8.8^
C / EC000.5	HA — Statistics	1 0.4^ 0.2>	5 2.0^ 0.8>	20 3.1^ 3.3>	28 4.3^ 4.6>	39 5.6^ 6.4>	36 3.2^ 5.9>	56 2.8^ 9.1>	120 2.3^ 19.6>	109 1.5^ 17.8>	83 1.6^ 13.5>	82 1.3^ 13.4.	29 0.9^ 4.7>	5 1.5^ 0.8>	613 1.8^
C / EC0026	HB — Economic Theory	12 5.0^ 0.4>	21 8.5^ 0.7>	83 12.7^ 2.9>	81 12.5^ 2.8>	86 12.3^ 3.0>	118 10.5^ 4.1>	187 9.3^ 6.4>	522 10.0^ 18.0>	652 9.0^ 22.5>	436 8.1^ 15.0>	487 7.6^ 16.8>	192 6.2^ 6.6>	24 7.2^ 0.8>	2901 8.7^
C / EC0031	HC — Economic History & Conditions National Production	8 3.3^ 0.1>	31 12.6^ 0.6>	116 17.8^ 2.1>	111 17.1^ 2.0>	104 14.9^ 1.9>	170 15.2^ 3.1>	376 18.7^ 6.9>	1011 19.3^ 18.4>	1336 18.5^ 24.3>	897 16.8^ 16.3>	976 15.2^ 17.8>	345 11.1^ 6.3>	6 1.8^ 0.1>	5487 16.5^
C / EC0037	HD1 — Economics - Production (Industrial Management)	6 2.5^ 0.3>	36 14.6^ 1.9>	22 3.4^ 1.2>	34 5.2^ 1.8>	39 5.6^ 2.0>	58 5.2^ 3.0>	99 4.9^ 5.2>	275 5.3^ 14.4>	405 5.6^ 21.2>	376 7.0^ 19.7>	378 5.9^ 19.8>	172 5.5^ 9.0>	8 2.4^ 0.4>	1908 5.7^
C / EC0040	HD2321 - 4730 — Economics - Industry	4 0.4>	12 1.7^ 1.3>	22 4.9^ 2.4>	28 3.4^ 3.0>	14 4.3^ 1.5>	36 2.0^ 3.9>	39 3.2^ 4.2>	108 1.9^ 11.6>	210 2.1^ 22.5>	145 2.9^ 15.6>	218 2.7^ 23.4>	88 3.4^ 9.4>	8 2.8^ 0.9>	932 2.4^
C / EC0044	HD4801 - 8942 — Labor	10 4.1^ 0.3>	9 3.7^ 0.3>	35 5.4^ 1.0>	63 9.7^ 1.8>	62 8.9^ 1.7>	121 10.8^ 3.4.	185 9.2^ 5.2>	638 12.2^ 18.0>	851 11.8^ 24.0>	598 11.2^ 16.9>	725 11.3^ 20.4>	235 7.5^ 6.6>	14 4.2^ 0.4>	3546 10.6^
C / EC0054	HD9000 - 999 — Special Industries & Trades	5 2.1^ 0.2>	7 2.8^ 0.2>	21 3.2^ 0.7>	32 4.9^ 1.1>	38 5.4^ 1.3>	66 5.9^ 2.3>	137 6.8^ 4.8>	365 7.0^ 12.9>	479 6.6^ 16.9>	631 11.8^ 22.3>	774 12.0^ 27.4>	259 8.3^ 9.2>	13 3.9^ 0.5>	2827 8.5^
C / EC0060	HE — Transportation & Communication	175 72.3^ 4.2>	47 19.1^ 1.1>	33 5.1^ 0.8>	44 6.8^ 1.1>	41 5.9^ 1.0>	70 6.3^ 1.7>	113 5.6^ 2.7>	289 5.5^ 7.0>	873 12.1^ 21.0>	660 12.3^ 15.9>	780 12.1^ 18.8>	864 27.7^ 20.8>	161 48.3^ 3.9>	4150 12.5^

Using The WLN Conspectus In A Non-Automated Environment

by Nancy Powell

Librarians nationwide agree that collection assessment is a valuable tool for managing the collection and allocating the materials budget. Libraries invariably list a variety of reasons for why an assessment is out of the question: "Yes, but. . .we're not automated." "We don't have enough staff, time, or resources, much less know-how to carry out an assessment." Or the time honored, "We've done projects like that before and no one really uses the information in the end." Despite being essentially excuses, all of these concerns are valid and bear some semblance of truth.

In spite of these concerns, libraries are assessing their collections and using the information to become better managers. Against all odds, Nicholls State University (NSU) Library completed 20 of the 24 Conspectus Divisions in ten months in a predominantly non-automated environment. The results of the assessment form the backbone of the NSU Ellender Memorial Library Collection Development Policy, the basis of the Library's materials budget allocation request to the University Administration, and a three-year collection management plan integrated into each Librarian's annual goals statement.

Blaine Hall has suggested that although libraries' objectives will vary considerably in any collection assessment program, in general they want to 1) evaluate the success of previous collection efforts, 2) monitor the ongoing collection program, and 3) provide empirical data for establishing priorities and allocating resources in order to achieve collection goals and objectives.(1)

This article will discuss why the WLN Conspectus was chosen as a collection assessment instrument, what worked and did not work for this mid-sized academic library, as well as adaptations of the Conspectus and enhancements to the process that were developed to complete the assessment and use the results.

PROBLEM STATEMENT

The NSU Library desperately needed a systematic process to manage their scarce resources. Methods and techniques for collecting and disseminating information about the strengths and weaknesses of the collection were needed. However, the librarians had very little training in collection management and virtually none in assessment techniques. Budget allocation was haphazard and erratic. In addition, the Library had only limited automation resources, such as a home-grown circulation system, OCLC cataloging, acquisitions, and ILL systems to provide support for the data gathering process.

In other words, like many smaller and medium-sized libraries nationwide, NSU needed the collection management information available from an assessment, but lacked the resources and organization needed to do an assessment.

BACKGROUND

Nicholls State University is a tax-supported, coeducational, regional university serving south central Louisiana as an accredited member of the

Nancy Powell is a consulting librarian in Albany, Oregon who has led collection assessment projects in Oregon, Washington, Texas, Massachusetts, and New Zealand. She was most recently Associate Director of the Library for the Ellender Memorial Library, Nicholls State University in Thibodaux, Louisiana. Before going to Louisiana, she was at Oregon State University for ten years. She holds an MLS from Louisiana State University.

Southern Association of Colleges and Schools. Renewal of accreditation was scheduled for 1995. Nicholls serves a relatively unsophisticated student population of approximately 7,000 undergraduate and graduate students from an area rich in tradition and culture, but generally economically depressed. Many Nicholls students are the first in their family to attend college. The scope of the mission of the University is very broad as it attempts to serve the educational needs of students from both the urban New Orleans area and the very rural bayou country. The University attempts to provide liberal learning as well as professional and technical education, primarily in the fields of education and teaching, nursing, and business administration.

Primary user groups of the Library are the students, faculty, and staff of the University. Of the 904 degrees awarded during the 1991-92 academic year, 215 were Associate, 617 were Bachelors, and 71 were Masters. Consequently, the collection focus is directed toward fulfilling the information needs of undergraduates first. The public is welcome to, and does use, the Library, but materials are not purchased specifically for this clientele.

The Library recognizes its special position as the only University library facility in a nine parish (county) area. The University and the Library are committed to the provision of limited service to a community of users defined by this nine parish area. Public libraries in the area are severely underfunded, and even though the University Library's funding for collection development has been erratic and unpredictable over the years, the collection remains the strongest in the area.

The collection includes approximately 193,000 catalogued titles in over 278,000 volumes; including books, serials, and government documents while excluding microforms. Current serial subscriptions number 1,815, with total titles numbering about 2,665. Uncataloged government documents arranged by SuDoc classification number approximately 500,000 units. Formats include paper, microforms, over 700 video tapes, slides, maps (6,000), a strong vertical file collection and over 3,000 linear feet of manuscripts and archives. The ratio of serials to monographs is about 50/50. However, government documents provide access to approximately one third of the collection. The Library receives about 66 percent of the total U. S. documents available to Depository Libraries.

OBJECTIVES

Faced with strongly conflicting demands for very scarce resources, the Library needed:

1. a systematic, objective means to allocate the resources available based on clearly defined program objectives;
2. a rationale to justify requests for additional funding for those areas of the collection that proved inadequate to the University's educational and research goals; and
3. a description of collection strengths and weaknesses to provide the background for a written collection development policy. The Library was criticized for having no written collection development policy during the previous accreditation study. The upcoming renewal increased the sense of urgency to complete the policy as soon as possible.

In the fall of 1992, the Library undertook an assessment of the collection in order to provide a description of the current collection, including an analysis of whether the collection and recent funding levels were adequate to support the curriculum and provide a rational basis for future collection development efforts.

Library administrators chose the WLN Conspectus as an assessment vehicle for several reasons. First it provides, via the Conspectus worksheets and methods, a systematic means for examining and describing the strengths and weaknesses of smaller to medium-sized collections. Second, it provides conspectus worksheets using the Dewey Classification scheme, which the NSU Library uses, as a guideline for locating materials. Third, the *WLN Collection Assessment Manual* provides numerous suggestions, techniques, explanations, worksheets, and helpful hints for gathering, organizing, and analyzing the data gathered.

INTRODUCTION OF COLLECTION ASSESSMENT OBJECTIVES AND TRAINING

All librarians at Nicholls hold subject assignment responsibility for monograph and non-print selection and provide recommendations to a serials committee for the selection of serials. The librarians generally work cooperatively with faculty representatives from subject related departments to make selections. However, the Library is responsible for the allocation and expenditure of the materials budget.

The first two major tasks of the project, clarifying the objectives of the collection assessment and training the staff in assessment techniques, proved much more time consuming than had been anticipated. Gathering the information is simple, even in a non-automated environment, compared to analyzing it to determine its significance. In addition, there was a general lack of understanding of how the information gathered would be used, and consequently a lack of motivation to complete the assessments, until departmental requests for accreditation information started flooding in about February. The assessment began to make sense when librarians could provide an overall description of the strengths of the collection compared to curricula and research needs. Using the information gathered to describe the collection was finally recognized as much more important than the data gathering techniques and processes.

The concept of determining the strengths and weaknesses of a collection is very complex. There are so many facets of a collection to consider. Since they were new tools, using the conspectus worksheets and collection code levels to present a summary description of the collection added to the librarians' confusion concerning what they were supposed to do to get from point A to point B (i.e., from data gathering to collection management). In spite of the fact that the *WLN Collection Assessment Manual* (2) was introduced as a resource to provide guidance and perspective on data gathering techniques,, most librarians took the project only one step at a time.

Difficulties, Problems, and Adaptations

Because the objectives of the project were limited in scope to providing information for collection management at NSU, and not part of a broader cooperative project, the assessment was limited to completing only those Divisions that were directly curriculum related.

One of the problems that surfaced fairly early in the project was that the Departments and/or curriculum frequently did not match the Conspectus Divisions and/or Categories. This made assigning a Division level collection code rating difficult, or even impossible, in some cases. For instance, the curriculum for the Psychology Department did not include Parapsychology, a section of the Conspectus and the collection. Some Departments, such as Nursing were only concerned with a very limited scope of the Division of Medicine. English and Foreign Languages are separate Departments, yet are included with the Division of Language, Linguistics, and Literature on the Conspectus worksheets. Because this project was a single institution project, unconnected to a cooperative project, the use of the Conspectus could be modified to meet specific Library needs in several ways.

In cases such as English and Foreign Languages, the Conspectus was completed as two separate sections, using the section appropriate to each subject collection. In the Medicine Division, only Nursing and Allied Health were

assessed at any real depth, with the other categories reported as "1a" or "NA". In the Business and Economics Division, Accounting was of such importance to the College of Business, that it was pulled out, assessed, and reported on at the Subject level. The *WLN Collection Assessment Manual* addresses several of these problems.

Another problem that arose centered around getting and agreeing on uniformly consistent baseline data such as acquisitions information (both in terms of how many titles were acquired and what figures should be used to calculate the costs), publishing output information, what constituted a valid sample size, and which lists to use for list checking. These questions were moderately difficult to resolve at the single institution level. In a cooperative project, skills in diplomacy, communication, and clarity are crucial to resolve these issues.

If an automated database and money are available, several commercial services can provide assistance with the assessment. One of the most labor intensive elements of an assessment is list checking. The "WLN BCL3 Collection Service" compares a library collection against the 3rd edition of *Books for College Libraries* and provides "Match, Close Match, and Miss" reports for a single library or a group of libraries. Libraries in Alaska and Montana have used this service effectively.

WLN also offers "Collection Analysis Reports" that match a library's or a group of libraries' machine-readable collection against the WLN or RLG Conspectus to provide subject analysis of the collection by publication date, material type, and other criteria. WLN and AMIGOS both provide "Title Overlap and Gap Analysis" services.

Comparable information about the number of monographs acquired by the NSU Library compared to the amount of dollars spent by curriculum subject areas was only available for the past five years. Interlibrary borrowing information regarding unfulfilled user demands on the collection was not available until the project began. However, the ILL staff was immediately responsive in developing a means to track borrowing so that information would be available in the future.

Annual circulation data was available for the past two years, but had to be summarized manually from the computer printouts. The question of whether or not to include "one time" bond money in the acquisitions expenditure had to be resolved. Almost everything from the number of titles to the median age of the collection had to be counted and calculated manually. Consequently, student workers had to be trained to gather data using consistent methods and measures.

Figure 1 illustrates the "Collection Management Summary Worksheet", a worksheet developed to guide data gathering activities. This worksheet proved useful for summarizing the information gathered whether the assessment was completed at the Category or Subject level of the Conspectus. It insured that all librarians gathered the same types of information, such as the number of titles and what percent each Category was of the Division as a whole. It further insured that information on all relevant formats was included, particularly serials, government documents, and non-print formats. (See Figure 1, "Collection Management Summary Worksheet".)

The "Program Focus" section of the worksheet provided an opportunity to indicate various levels of curricula and research need, for instance which Categories were part of the undergraduate core program and which supported research or graduate level needs within a Division. Student enrollment levels, which may indicate potential demand on the collection, were recorded in the "Demographics" section.

The "Red Flags Comments" note discrepancies between user needs as indicated in the Circulation, ILL, Demographics, and Program Focus sections as well as collection strengths or weaknesses. This was the point at which an analysis of the collection began. Librarians recorded recommendations for collection management in the final column, "Action/Changes Needed", to bring the collection into congruence with user needs.

The original idea for this chart was developed jointly by the author and Mary Bushing in 1990 while working with the Cape and Islands Interlibrary Association libraries on Cape Cod, Massachusetts. A number of the elements in the chart, included in the *WLN Collection Assessment Manual* (3), have since been incorporated into the WLN Conspectus software.

COLLECTION ASSESSMENT NARRATIVE SUMMARY

NSU began the Southern Association accreditation renewal Self-Study in 1993. As mentioned earlier, using assessment information to describe the strengths and weaknesses of the collection is one of the reasons for undertaking such a project. The collection assessment project resulted in a comprehensive Collection Development Policy, which is required of the Library for the University's accreditation Self-Study.

At about the same time, professional accrediting agencies and the University Administration were both asking for documentation concerning how well the Library supported programs under review. The charge to the Departments from the University was to "describe whether or not suffi-cient library materials and databases exist to support the department's educational, research, and public service programs. Evaluate whether or not the Library's collection for graduate work in your area is substantially beyond the requirement for the baccalaureate work."

It was determined that a narrative summary report, supported by the appropriate Conspectus worksheets, was needed to address the questions raised for accreditation renewals and the Departmental reviews. The narrative summary report, as illustrated in Appendix A, addressed the collection primarily at the Division level. This was done by comparing a description of Departmental program needs to a description of the collection. The comparison was based on degrees offered and courses core to the curriculum, primary and secondary users, and minimum expected demand on the collection based on the number of student credit hours for each Department.

The description of the collection included the following elements:

Description of the monograph collection:
- number of titles and median age/subject area by category level class number
- total number of titles and median age overall
- median age of the reference collection
- language(s) represented
- physical description—including percent of textbooks and multiple copies
- qualitative description including comparison to appropriate lists such as BCL3, noted strengths and/or weaknesses
- percent of annual circulation
- acquisition commitment including: Dollars spent/yr. over the last four years and a comparison to publishing output

Description of the serials collection:
- number of subject related titles held in all formats
- description of the extent of runs
- number of titles of subject specific Indexes and Abstracts
- number of general CD or online access (such as *InfoTrac*)
- Comparison of holdings to appropriate lists such as *Magazines for Libraries* including a description of the ratio of undergraduate to graduate level literature
- description of categories most strongly supported

Description of other formats:
- number of video titles
- description of the strength of the Government Documents collection relevant to the Division including a brief description of the type of

information found in different agency reports relevant to the subject area; the names of particularly relevant agencies and the related class number (SuDoc) for instance ERIC for Education; and the number of titles held by relevant agencies

Description of interdisciplinary support, cooperative relationships, off-campus sites, and ILL support

Present Collection Level
- "sufficient" or "insufficient" to support program demands with a Division Level rating (e.g. 3a), including the definition of that rating from the *Manual*

Recommended Collection Goal Level needed to support the program using Conspectus ratings and definitions

Summary of collection management action needed to bring the collection in line with program demands

The narrative summary proved valuable for elaborating on the significance of particular sections of a subject collection. For instance, in the Psychology collection, the strength of the collection was diminished by the age, physical condition, and number of old textbooks and duplicates in the monograph collection. However, this disparity was balanced by the strength of the serials collection which contained 40 percent of the titles recommended in *Magazines for Libraries* and 15 of the 17 recommended titles published by the American Psychological Association.

The narrative summary statements were sent to each Department at the end of May to meet their accreditation report needs. In addition, the assessments served as an excellent communication tool to foster dialog between the subject librarians and the Departmental faculty for setting collection management priorities. Library administrators used the assessment findings to begin the process of budget reallocation and new budget request justification with the Provost.

Finally, each librarian completed a "Collection Management Plan" for each subject area under his or her responsibility to guide selection and collection management activities for the next three years (see Appendix B) (4). These plans were then integrated into the librarians' annual goals statements.

Many libraries have used, and are using, the WLN Conspectus to guide, document, and present their assessment results. The narrative summary provided a means for integrating the collection assessment information into the collection development policy in a user-friendly manner. (Appendix C includes the Table of Contents of the Collection Development Policy indicating the role of the narrative summary within the Policy.) Used in conjunction with the narrative summary, the conspectus reports became much more readily acceptable as a concise communication tool to describe the strengths and weaknesses of the Categories and Subjects of the collection within a particular Division.

CONCLUSION AND RECOMMENDATIONS

A comprehensive collection assessment project is a complex, time consuming process that requires a strong commitment on the part of administrators and librarians alike if it is to be successful, but the benefits far outweigh the costs. Leadership, based on a clear vision of how the results will be used, is the single most important element to the success of the project. It is absolutely essential that the objectives of the project are clearly understood by the professional staff involved at the very least. Ownership of the project by all concerned promotes problem solving and an attitude of cooperation.

The WLN Conspectus proved to be an effective tool for assessing the collection because it provided both a systematic means of review and a standardized vocabulary for describing the strengths and weaknesses of the collection.

The NSU collection assessment project accomplished the stated goals. The librarians developed a systematic process for managing the collection and making objective recommendations for funding requests. The Division level narrative summaries and Conspectus reports provided a means to describe the strengths and weaknesses of the collection for accreditation reports and Departmental reviews. Perhaps the most important achievement of all was that the librarians learned techniques for managing the ongoing collection program, and gained confidence in their ability to interpret the collection's strengths and weaknesses to its users.

The use of commercial automated services is efficient and will save staff time in gathering statistics about the collection—especially list checking. However, there is no substitute for the professional expertise of librarians who will analyze the assessment findings for their relevance and significance to the decision making process while taking responsibility for using the results in collection management activities.

Figure I

COLLECTION MANAGEMENT
SUMMARY WORKSHEET

Subject Division	Class Number	BOOKS										SERIALS			
		Titles		Median Age	List Check		BPO	Acquisition		Circulation		ILL		Curr. Sub.		List Check	
		#	%		#	%		#	%	#	%	#	%	#	%	#	%

COLLECTION MANAGMENT
SUMMARY WORKSHEET
Page 2

Gov. Docs. # / Agency	Other Formats #	User Demographics	Program Focus	"Red Flag Comments"	Actions/Changes Needed

SAMPLE NARRATIVE SUMMARY

Psychology

Description of the Program

The University awards the *Bachelor of Arts* degree with a major in Psychology. The study of Psychology has a two-fold purpose: 1) to help the students better understand their behavior and that of others, and 2) to give valuable foundation training for such vocations such as teaching and school administration, homemaking, social work, business, personnel and counseling work, and mental health centers.

Students may complete a minor in Psychology by taking the following courses in Psychology:

- •101 **General Psychology:** Human behavior from the mental, physical, and emotional standpoint.
- •204 **Psychology of Personality:** Emphasizes the development and structure of personality.
- •211 **Social Psychology:** Stresses individual and interpersonal relationships; cultural forces as they effect attitude, social learning, perception, and communication of the individual and group.
- •208 **Statistics:** Introduces descriptive and inferential statistical methods.
- •301 **Abnormal Psychology:** Discusses the dynamics of abnormal disorders of psychological origin.
- •302 **Psychological Measurement:** Treats the administration and interpretation of tests of intelligence, aptitude, interests, and personality.
- •402 **Psychology of Counseling:** Discusses the theories of counseling and their applications to educational, social-welfare agencies, mental health, and private practice.

The University awards the *Master of Arts* degree in Psychological Counseling; and the *Master of Education* degree in Counselor Education and Specialist in School Psychology.

Undergraduate preparation for the *Psychological Counseling* program includes course work in General Psychology, Statistics and Experimental/Research Design, Measurement, Abnormal, Personality, Developmental, Learning, History and Systems, Social, Counseling Theories, and Physiological Psychology. Graduate course work requires a 48 hour emphasis.

The curriculum for certification as an elementary or secondary school counselor includes 12 hours of graduate level course work in Psychology at the 500 level.

Undergraduate preparation for the "Specialist in School Psychology" program includes 18 hours of undergraduate psychology in statistics, research methods, psychological measurement, physiological psychology, and psychology of exceptional children. Graduate course work requires 60 academic hours.

Primary users of the Library's collection in Psychology are undergraduates, both interdisciplinary and majors, graduate majors and faculty. Psychology is an option for fulfilling the core requirement in Social Sciences. As such, it provides support for undergraduate programs across the University, as well as providing support for graduate programs in Education.

The number of student credit hours for each department has been used as a uniform measure of the minimum demand placed on the Library's collections and services. Psychology majors accounted for approximately 9,912 out of 202,275 Student Credit Hours for 1991-92 or roughly 4.9 percent of total student credit hours.

Description of the collection
Monograph Collection:

The approximate number of cataloged books and the median age of the circulating collection that supports Psychology follows: **(Table 1 reference)**

The *Psychology* collection contains *5699* monographic titles or *3 percent* of the total collection. The median age of the circulating collection is approximately *1965-74*. The median age of the Reference collection for this subject area is approximately *1985-89*. The collection is almost exclusively in English.

Physical examination of the monograph collection:
Circulating collection

In general, the monograph collection is *old*. The collection is in desperate need of weeding. Weeding the old, worn, musty, superseded materials will enhance the collection's reputation for reliability and encourage circulation by making the collection more attractive and up-to-date for students. Shelves which are crowded with worn, out-of-date materials discourage students looking for a particular book and cost staff time in reshelving and locating the good sources that are available.

Several sections in particular are weighted down with old textbooks. These sections include: the beginning section of General Psychology; the section on "study and teaching" (Dewey 150.7); the whole section on "Subconscious and Altered States and Processes" (154); the section on "Child Psychology", "Psychology of Young Adults", and "Psychology of Adults" (155.4-.6); and the section on "Applied Psychology" (158).

TABLE 1

SUBJECT AREA	DEWEY CLASS NO.	TITLES	AGE
Paranormal Phenomena	130	0	—
Psychology	150	828	65-74
Sensory Perception/Movement/Emotions	152	506	65-74
Conscious Mental Processes & Intelligence	153	690	65-74
Subconscious & Altered States & Process	154	92	55-64
Differential & Genetic Psychology	155	1748	65-74
Comparative Psychology	156	103	65-74
Applied Psychology	158	506	75-79
Educational Psychology	370.15	552	65-74
diseases: suicide, mental retardation, alcohol & drug addict, insanity	616.858-.89	552	65-74
(this section absorbs Abnormal and Clinical Psychology Dewey 157)			

In addition to the problems with old textbooks, the section on "Child Psychology", "Psychology of Young Adults", and "Psychology of Adults" also contains numerous multiple copies of old books.

The collection includes some classic materials and authoritative works such as a series on the *History of Psychology*, a new set on Freud (1989), a concordance to the standard edition of the *Complete Psychological Works of Sigmund Freud*, and works by Jung, Adler, Rorschach, Piaget, Maslow, Theodore Reik, Erik Erikson, Kurt Koffka, and others.

Reference collection

The Reference collection is newer with more strength in general psychology, testing and mental measurement, and "differential and genetic" (child and adolescent) psychology. Nevertheless, this area is in need of selection focus.

Qualitative Description:

A comparison of our overall book collection holdings in Psychology to *Books for College Libraries*, 3rd, a core list of titles recommended for a college library, reveals that the Library holds approximately 28 percent of the recommended titles from a random sample. The recommended titles held come from across the entire list, more

or less. Our weakest holdings of recommended titles fell in the areas of "psychology of the unconscious" and parapsychology. Titles included are scholarly works by noted authorities and are relevant to the NSU program.

Circulation:

Annual circulation statistics for FY 1991-92 indicate *light* use of Psychology books, approximately 4.2 percent of total book circulations for 1990-92. The heaviest use is in the areas of general psychology, Conscious Mental Processes/Intelligence, Differential and Genetic Psychology (child and adolescent), and Applied Psychology.

Acquisition Commitment:

The amount spent on this subject area for books for the last four years compared to the total amount of state dollars spent by the Library is summarized below: **Table 2 Reference**

Annual US book publication for materials in Psychology as reflected in the *Bowker Annual* is approximately 1.2 percent of total publication or approximately 600 books per year. The Library acquired with state funding an average of approximately 114 books/year, or roughly 19 percent, of the number published annually in Psychology. The bond funding certainly improved

TABLE 2

1989–90	1990–91	1991–92	1992–93	Total
State $	State/Bond $	State/Bond $ State $	State + Bond	% State
5,662	4,723/1,827	432/1,4531,200	12,017+15,296	**3.8%**

the collection but should be reflected as "one time only." Of the total amount spent by the Library over this four year period, 3.8 percent was dedicated to Psychology. This is a low rate of funding support compared to roughly 4.9 percent SCH for this subject area.

Description of the Serials Collection:

The Library's serials collection contains 2353 titles in paper format and 322 titles in microform. The collection contains 95 serial titles (approximately 3.6%) which directly support the Psychology. Serial runs are generally *continuous*.

Basic recommended abstracts and indexes for this subject include: *Biological Abstracts* (available online via Dialog), *Psychological Abstracts*, and *Index Medicus*. Additional indexes which support this subject area that the Library subscribes to include: *Current Index of Journals in Education, Education Index, Social Sciences Index, Child Development Abstracts, Nutrition Abstracts and Reviews: Series A, Sociological Abstracts*, and *Public Affairs Information Services*.

In addition to these specific indexes, the Library subscribes to *Infotrac*, a general academic periodical index on CD-ROM.

A comparison of the periodical titles held by NSU relevant to the Psychology program, to titles in the core list (*Magazines for Libraries* by Katz) indicate that the Library subscribes to approximately *40 percent* of the titles recommended. In addition, the Library holds 15 of the 17 recommended titles published by the American Psychological Association which "represent a number of basic journals supporting professors, practitioners, and graduate students in the field of psychology." Katz recommends that libraries supporting research in the psychological sciences should have most of these titles. Of the recommended titles that the Library holds, approximately two-thirds are basic academic journals, with one-third being suitable for more advanced professional research.

The Psychology serials are concentrated mostly in the areas of General Psychology (10.5%), Differential and Genetic Psychology (9.5%), and from the medical area of Diseases: mental disorders such as suicide, mental retardation, alcohol and drug addiction and insanity (19%).

Description of Other Formats Including AV and Government Documents:

Video Holdings: A review of the Library's *List of Video Holdings* indicates the availability of approximately *41* video tapes related to Psychology.

Documents: The Psychology collection is strengthened by our collection of federal documents. The Library receives 66 percent of U.S.

Government publications available to the public. The Government Documents unit of the Library houses documents which support the Psychology program primarily from the Health and Human Services Department, Education Department, and Defense Department. Because of the interdisciplinary nature of the subject, many other agencies also publish documents which may be relevant to Psychology. Access to Government Documents is available through the *Monthly Catalog* and through the "Government Publications" index on *Infotrac*.

Approximately 1,575 titles in paper and 225 in microfiche from the National Institute of Mental Health subunit of the Health and Human Services Department (HHS) directly support Psychology. Some of the other subunits of HHS providing documents in support of Psychology include the "National Institutes of Health" (HE 20.30), "National Center for Health Statistics" (HE 20.6209),"National Institute for Occupational Safety and Health" (HE 20.71), and "Alcohol, Drug Abuse, and Mental Health Administration" (HE 20.80). Some of the subunits of the Education Department are "National Center for Educational Statistics" (ED 1.1), "Educational Research and Improvement Office" (ED 1.310), and "Programs for the Handicapped" (ED 1.31).

The Defense Department produces numerous documents based on psychological research related to both health issues and education and training of recruits. A selection of some of the types of documents relevant to Psychology that are available from the Library's documents collection can be found in Appendix A.

ERIC (ED 1.3): The Psychology collection is significantly strengthened by our *ERIC* (Educational Resources Information Center) documents collection on microfiche. ERIC collects and disseminates virtually all types of print materials, many unpublished, that deal with education and/or related fields from a variety of sources (journal articles, research reports, conference papers, bibliographies, innovative practice reports, chapters from books, and other printed forms). Indexes are published monthly with two bi-annual publications. NSU holds the complete ERIC file on microfiche, and the indexes in paper. Our holdings number more than 366,000 titles.

Interdisciplinary Considerations

The collection is appreciably strengthened by the Library's collections in the areas of Education, Nursing, Sociology, and Business.

Present Collection Level

The scope, depth and median age of the

monograph collection is very weak; *insufficient* to support the demands of a Baccalaureate or Master's level program. A comparison of the collection to a core list of titles recommended for college libraries revealed that the collection includes the most important primary and secondary literature and the basic reference and bibliographical tools for the subject. With updating and weeding, the collection is adequate to support lower division undergraduate course work.

The current acquisition commitment is at the "Intermediate Study or Instructional Support Level" (3b). (These American Library Association recognized collection levels are more fully defined in Appendix B.)

With consideration given to the Government Documents Collection including ERIC, the strong Serials collection, and the audio visual collection, the present collection is judged to be *sufficient* to support all but the Master's degree programs in Psychology.

Collection Level Goal Level

The overall collection level adequate to support the educational programs in the Psychology department should be between a *(3b-3c)* collection level. An *"Intermediate Study or Instructional Support Level (3b) "* collection level "provides resources adequate for imparting and maintaining knowledge about the basic or primary topics of a subject area. The collection includes a broad range of basic works in appropriate formats, classic retrospective materials, all key journals on primary topics, selected journals and seminal works on secondary topics, access to appropriate machine-readable data files, and the referenced tools and fundamentals bibliographical apparatus pertaining to the subject. These materials are adequate to support advanced undergraduate course work. It is not adequate to support master's degree programs".

Summary

In order to adequately support the curriculum at both the undergraduate and graduate level, the focus of the collection should be on general psychology (Dewey 150), "Sensory Perception/Movement/Emotions" (152), "Conscious Mental Processes & Intelligence" (153), "Applied Psychology" (158), and "Abnormal and Clinical Psychology" (616.858—.89).

If the current acquisition commitment remains consistent for books and serials, and a weeding program is implemented, the collection level can be expected to stabilize at a solid 3b level for monographs and serials. Selection focus for the monograph collection for the next several years needs to concentrate first on improving the Reference collection, weeding the circulating collection, and working with the faculty to target those areas of the collection that warrant first priority to support graduate level study.

Conspectus Database Worksheet—Dewey

Library:
Date: By:

Division : PSYCHOLOGY

DEWEY CLASS	LINE NUMBER	DIVISION AND CATEGORIES	CL	AC	GL	PC	COMMENTS
	PSD000	PSYCHOLOGY	3b	3b	3b		5699 books, 3% total collection; M.A. = 65-74; predominantly Eng. lang.; 28% BCL3 recommended titles; old, worn physical condition; approximately 1800 docs.
130-139	PSD005	Paranormal Phenomena	NA	NA	NA		0 titles
150	PSD010	Psychology (20th: formerly also 159)	3a	NA	3b		828 book titles; M.A. = 65. 74; 39% BCL3; heavy to old textbooks; 17% circ; core LD; 10 serials weed. Purchase core focus; docs strength
152	PSD020	Sensory Percep/Movement/Emotions/Physiological Dr.	3a	NA	3b		502 books; M.A. = 65. 74; 8% BCL3; 8% circ; 7 serials core & grad focus; weed; purchase focus
153 (20th: also 153.9)	PSD030	Conscious Mental Processes & Intelligence	3a	NA	3b		698 books; M.A. = 65-74; 20% BCL3; 12% circ; docs strength; core & grad focus; 3 serials; weed books!
154	PSD040	Subconscious & Altered States & Processes	1b	NA			92 books; MA = 55-64; 0 serials; 4.5% circ; heavy to old textbooks; weed textbooks; buy very selectively
155	PSD050	Differential & Genetic Psychology (20th: formerly 155.28 Comprehensive works on testing & measurement in differential & developmental & psychology only; 16th: 136)	3b	NA	3c		1761 books; MA = 65-74; 22% BCL3; 33% circ! 9 serials; heavy to old textbooks & dups: weed! buy books! consider serials; good docs support ED/HE
156	PSD060	Comparative Psychology	1b	NA			103 books; MA = 65-74; .5% BCL3; 1.6% circ 1 serials; limited buying only
158	PSD080	Applied Psychology (19th: formerly 131.3)	3a	NA	3c		506 books; MA = 75-79; 3% BCL3; 13% circ; buy books! 7 serials; docs ED 1.3; heavy to old textbooks; purchase focus: core & grad. level
616.858		ABNORMAL PSYCHOLOGY	3b				621 books; MA = 65-74; academic focus, never/better collection; 19 serials; core & grad focus
370.15		EDUCATIONAL PSYCHOLOGY	3a		3c		552 books; MA = 65-74; 9 serials; master's program focus; buy!

Collection Planning Worksheet

Use a collection planning for such as this to plan changes for identified needs in the collection. Those needs may be to maintain strength, to week, to acquire, to move—to act upon each subject segment in some meaningful manner. Below is a possible format for such planning, with large spaces provided for planning specific actions to take with the collection over a period of three years.

SUBJECT/NEED	CLASS #	YEAR #1	YEAR #2	YEAR #3
STATISTICS	310-319	begin purchasing missing areas	ibid., buy "best books" plus core items	ibid.
ECON.	330	weed multiples; textbooks pre-'75	focus on critiques; secondary sources	pick up gaps in classical works
LABOR ECON.	331	weed extensively	buy books on labor in '80s-'90s	buy on world labor situation/projections
FINANCIAL ECON.	332	weed extensively; buy as a high priority	spend a large % in this field.	begin to cut back if collection improves
LAND ECONOMICS	333	purchase core titles	purachase core if necessary	weed if necessary
COOPERATIVES	334	slight spending	slight spending	
SOCIALISM	335	weed carefully; buy classics	buy critiques, secondary sources	buy secondary sources
PUBLIC FINANCE	336	weed extensively; purchase large %	major purchasing focus	ibid.
INTL. ECON.	337	purchase a large %	ibid.	re-evaluate collection
PRODUCTION	338	weed; maintain current spending	maintain spending	ibid.
MACROECONOMICS	339	minimal weeding	no further action needed	
INSURANCE	368	weed extensively; top spending priority	top spending priority	ibid.
COMMERCE, COMM.	380	slight weeding, keep spending at level	ibid.	ibid.
INTERNAL COMMERCE	381	slight weeding; keep spending at level	ibid.	ibid.
INTERNATIONAL COMM.	382	weed extensively; major spending focus	spend large %	ibid.
POSTAL COMMUNICATION	383	minor purchasing	ibid.	no action
TELECOMMUNI-CATIONS	384	spend larger % on future trends	ibid.	ibid., if needed
RAILROAD TRANSP.	385	weed; spend minimal amount	spend, look for future	trends, innovations

APPENDIX C

Table of Contents

PREFACE
COLLECTION DEVELOPMENT POLICY
I. GENERAL INTRODUCTION
    A. Mission Statement
    B. Audiences and Purposes of the Policy
    C. Community Analysis and User Groups Description
    D. Description of the Types of Programs and Patron Needs
    E. Overview of the Collection
    F. Cooperative Collection Development
II. GENERAL COLLECTION MANAGEMENT PRINCIPLES AND LIMITATIONS
    A. Scope of Collections—Currency, Historical Emphasis
    B. Formats and Languages
    C. Special Funding to Be Considered
    D. Organization of Collection Development Responsibilities and Processes
    E. General Selection Criteria
    F. Gift Policy
    G. Collection Maintenance
    H. Complaints and/or Reconsideration of Materials
    I. Limits or Restrictions
III. NARRATIVE STATEMENTS FOR SPECIAL COLLECTIONS OR FORMATS
    A. Separate or Restricted Collections
    B. Format Collections
IV. DETAILED ANALYSIS OF SUBJECT COLLECTIONS
    A. Aeronautical Science
    B. Agricultural Sciences
    C. Art
    D. Biology
    E. Business Administration
    F. Chemistry
    G. Computer Science
    H. Earth Science and Geography
    I. Education
    J. Engineering Technology & Petroleum Services
    K. English
    L. Foreign Languages
    M. Government (Criminal Justice, Paralegal, Sociology)
    N. Health & Physical Education
    O. History
    P. Home Economics (in Engineering & Technology Conspectus)
    Q. Mass Communications (Communications and Journalism)
    R. Mathematics
    S. Music
    T. Nursing
    U. Office of Information Systems (in Business Conspectus)
    V. Physics
    W. Psychology
    X. Speech and Hearing
V. POLICY IMPLEMENTATION, EVALUATION AND REVISION

References

1. Blaine H. Hall, *Collection Assessment Manual for College and University Libraries.* (Phoenix: Oryx Press, 1985), 1.
2. Nancy Powell and Mary Bushing. *WLN Collection Assessment Manual,* 4th ed. (Lacey, WA: WLN, 1992).
3. Ibid., 67.
4. Ibid., 68.

Shared Futures: Cooperative Collection Development And Management In Alaska

by June Pinnell-Stephens

Since its inception in 1982, the tasks of the Alaska Collection Development project have changed as technology and our understanding of the process evolved and grew, but the goal has never varied. We strive to become more effective stewards of our limited library and information resources.

ENVIRONMENT

Contrary to common perception, Alaska is very poor in resources, at least in terms of its libraries:

- In 1983, Paul Mosher, then at Stanford University Libraries, estimated that the combined holdings of every library in Alaska was about one-third that of the Stanford libraries.
- In 1988, the Collection Development Steering Committee, the group from four academic, three public, one school, and one special library and the State Library, calculated that the combined monograph budgets of every major library in Alaska were about equal to that of the library at Oregon State University.
- The ten members of the Steering Committee represent libraries that hold more than 75 percent of Alaska's library resources.

It's fortunate that Alaskans were already inclined by their frontier nature to share, because there simply was no option—none of the libraries could come close to fulfilling the library and information needs of its patrons alone. It was in this environment of limited resources that the Alaska CD Project began.

HISTORY

In 1981, Dennis Stephens, Collection Development Officer at Rasmuson Library, University of Alaska Fairbanks, attended the RTSD Institute on Collection Development and Management at Stanford University. He returned with a vision of how coordinating collections could be applied to small libraries with extremely limited resources, as well as to the major research libraries that had begun the process, and wrote a successful grant under the Alaska State Library's Interlibrary Cooperation Program. The State Library, recognizing the potential benefits of cooperative collection development, has continued to fund the activities of the Steering Committee for the past 11 years. Needless to say, their support has been critical to the success of the program.

The goal of the project, as recorded in the Alaska Coordinated Collection Development Agreement, was then and remains to this day "to eliminate unnecessary duplication of purchases in order to broaden the base of materials available within participating libraries," and "is based on the following principles:

- Each library requires a core collection of materials available locally to support its fundamental mission.

June Pinnell-Stephens is Collection Development Librarian, Fairbanks North Star Borough Public Library, and Coordinator of the Alaska Conspectus Consortium. She is past President of the Alaska Library Association and the Pacific Northwest Library Association and is former Chair of the Alaska Collection Development Steering Committee. She received her MLS from the University of Washington in 1972.

- For each library, reduction of purchases in some areas can be made with confidence that these subject areas are being covered adequately by another library, and funds thus released will be reallocated to build stronger backup collections in chosen areas of specialization which all libraries may share.
- Libraries which coordinate resource sharing and collection development will be able to offer collectively more materials more cost-effectively than any one of the libraries could provide individually."[1]

The first grant brought in Paul Mosher as the consultant. He brought with him the question, "If we don't know what our resources are, how can we plan them, manage them, or lend them?"[2] He also brought the Conspectus as a way to answer that question. (Please see Sally Loken's article in this volume for a description of the Conspectus and the assessment process.) The Steering Committee took the RLG Conspectus, adapted it somewhat to make it easier to apply to small libraries, and used it to assess their collections.

The Committee then had to find a home for its data in order to manipulate and use it. The first attempt involved a hot-shot student hacker on an Apple, who found the project to be more daunting than he'd anticipated. Fortunately, about that time, the Fred Meyer Charitable Trust launched its Library and Information Resources for the Northwest (LIRN) Program, and the Northwest Conspectus, borrowing from the Alaska model, began to develop. A more complete discussion of the development and activities of the Alaska project can be found in the article "Multi-type Library Collection Planning in Alaska: a Conspectus-Based Approach" by Dennis Stephens.

COOPERATIVE AGREEMENTS

All of the libraries represented on the Steering Committee have now been assessed in nearly all of the conspectus divisions, and the data is now part of the WLN database as the Alaska Conspectus Consortium. On the basis of collection strengths determined by the assessment process and reported from the database, Committee members have assumed primary or secondary collecting responsibility in subject areas appropriate for their libraries. These commitments form the *Alaska Cooperative Collection Development Agreement*, which will be submitted to the directors for their signatures upon its' completion. A sample page of this agreement can be found in Appendix A.

The process of writing the Agreement was valuable both for learning about resources statewide and for understanding how individual institutions contributed to those resources. It was, for example, sobering to realize that no library in Alaska had a large enough base collection (nominally 3a) combined with sufficient acquisition commitment to assume primary responsibility for collecting in any category of the Anthropology, Chemistry, Computer Science, Geography, Music, Performing Arts, Philosophy, Physical Sciences, and Sociology divisions, much less one of these divisions as a whole.

However, the agreement provided a basis for making decisions about specific items and whole collections, individually and collectively. For example, I skip most titles in library science, because the State Library has primary responsibility for that division, but purchase heavily in parapsychology and the occult, because my library has primary responsibility for that area of the Psychology Division. And when the State Library changed from a general collection of materials to one supporting the needs of state government only, the general collection was redistributed primarily on the basis of statewide collecting responsibilities. Finally, the academic libraries examined duplicate serials in view of their collecting responsibilities and made substantial adjustments in their subscriptions. They also participated in a cooperative purchase with the Northwest Canadian Studies Consortium, locating segments of the entire collection in different libraries and indexes in all of them.

Of even greater immediate impact are the local collecting and other cooperative agreements developed subsequently in the three population centers:

In Juneau, the Capitol Cities Libraries agreement includes the university, the public library, one high school, and the State Library in a jointly shared catalog and circulation system, courier service, and coordinated purchasing program based on their Conspectus data and collecting responsibilities.

In Fairbanks, the North Star Libraries agreement augments the reciprocal borrowing agreement and subject-level collecting responsibilities by targeting specific resources for each library; e.g., the public library doesn't compete for rare Alaskana and the university library no longer collects juvenile books. As a result, students in a university course in children's literature rely on the public library's collection. This agreement has also resulted in a transfer of resources from one library to another to reflect our collecting responsibilities, an example being the public library's planned relocation of its genealogy collection to the local Latter Day Saints church library.

The libraries in Anchorage are beginning to address the issues of reciprocal borrowing and courier service in their LINK project.

Despite progress in implementing cooperative agreements, members of the Steering Committee have expressed concern about their effectiveness. Have we, in fact, lived up to the collecting priorities we've assumed so far? Are the agreements doing what we'd hoped they would? How can we tell?

COLLECTION MANAGEMENT

Those of us who assessed our libraries gained invaluable knowledge about our collections. We found the holes, acknowledged the strengths, and discovered the surprises. If we went to the shelves for the assessment, which many of us had never done before, we also got some idea of the collection's use and condition. In most cases, we planned all stages of the assessing activity carefully. However, we didn't realize that the assessments and the cooperative agreements they made possible were only the first steps. We could not have predicted the number of questions the Conspectus process and the resulting agreements would raise, e.g., "What does a 3a acquisition commitment in this subject mean in dollars" and "Is a goal level of 3b adequate for collection use and ILL activity in this area?"

In order to address these and other questions, the Research and Resource Library Directors in Alaska asked the Steering Committee to design a method of analyzing collections through use of the Conspectus that would compare collection strengths and limitations against each library's circulation, clientele, institutional missions, and, in the case of academic libraries, curriculum. In addition, the Steering Committee calculated benchmark budget amounts necessary to meet collection responsibilities. Since this analysis was intended to build on the assessment work already completed by using the Conspectus as a structure, the Committee began working with WLN to help design what has become a management information system, or MIS, for collections. My library was one of three beta sites and the system is now a part of WLN's Conspectus Database Software.

Much like other management information systems, its goal is to provide "past, present, and projection information. . .relating to. . .internal operations and. . .environment. It supports the managers. . .by furnishing information in the proper time frame to assist in decision making."[3] The key elements that differentiate an MIS from a machine analysis, such as a *BCL3* (*Books for College Libraries*, 3d ed.) comparison, are:

1. The ability to link past and present information with the projection information built into the Conspectus through the acquisition commitment and goal levels.
2. The ability to connect collections with other internal and external factors.

For a more complete discussion of the MIS process and the WLN Management file, please see my article, "President's Forward. After Assessment: Building on the Conspectus for Management Information."

In applying the MIS process to collection development, the problem is almost universal—there isn't enough money to buy everything, and the funds available must be spent as effectively as possible. Objectives, however, will vary from library to library in order to reflect individual and/or consortium priorities. Depending on the data entered in the WLN Collection Management file, it is possible to answer such questions as:

- Are there subject areas in which the circulation or curriculum doesn't justify the amount we're spending?
- Are there subject areas for which the ILL activity indicates we may be spending too much or too little for our cooperative collecting responsibility?
- How do our acquisition figures and holdings compare to other universities with similar student FTE who received accreditation for their School of Engineering?
- How many of the titles listed in *Public Library Catalog* or *BCL3* in psychology do we have and how much would it cost us, based on our average cost per title in that division, to achieve 100 percent coverage?

Determining objectives—i.e., deciding which questions to ask—is the crux of the process. The WLN file offers 15 pre-determined fields of data—circulation, ILL borrowed, ILL lent, titles purchased, amount spent on books, amount spent on journals, volumes added, volumes deleted, total volumes held, number on a recommended list, journals held, journals published, and books published in last five years—plus ten user-defined fields. They all require a certain amount of work to obtain the data in a useable structure, but very few libraries will want or need to use them all, at least immediately. Deciding which of these fields are necessary to answer specific questions is critical for the success of the project.

When determining feasibility, the area most likely to be a problem is the data. And the problem is not that there is a lack of it. We're inundated with data. The problem is that library reports—circulation, ILL, acquisitions, etc.—are typically organized using different structures, and the challenge is translating them to the same structure (in this case the Conspectus, so they can be compared). The newer automated systems should allow design of reports that sort circulation and possibly acquisitions data into Conspectus divisions and categories using call number ranges. For those that don't, or for data not available from automated sources, remember that in the Conspectus, as in horseshoes, close counts. That statement may sound cavalier, but reconciling five different systems to one structure is no time to be compulsive. It is important to recognize that although some of the data may be approximate, it is still useable for both individual and cooperative projects.

LESSONS

In the beginning, adoption of the Conspectus methodology was a leap of faith—anything so intuitively correct must, at least eventually, be helpful. Committee members discovered the benefits of assessing their own collections and possibly those of their colleagues in team efforts. We built cooperative agreements based on those assessments. Over time, we came to recognize that it is not necessary, or even appropriate, to involve every participating library in every decision. Some agreements can only be implemented at the local level or among similar types of libraries. That recognition, however, did not negate the importance of maintaining the multitype, statewide Conspectus-based structure we adopted. And now, with the addition of the Management file, there is a comprehensive view for expanding our understanding and answering the questions raised in the initial process.

Last year, my library began using the Management file. Even though the information will only be truly meaningful over time, or in comparison to other libraries, the results from that first year's data clearly indicated necessary adjustments to traditional budget allocations. This year, we'll be able to determine if purchasing decisions have reflected the acquisition commitments in the assessment and we'll have a concrete picture of the impact of a static materials budget. We'll also be able to evaluate the effect of a Library Services and Construction Act Foreign Language Materials grant by changes in circulation, ILL, and assessment levels. (In the award notice for that grant, all three peer evaluators commented on the use of the Conspectus; both to assess the need for and to evaluate the success of the project.)

If the Conspectus is the basis for establishing

cooperative agreements, then the Management file can be the means of verifying and monitoring their effectiveness. When data from the other participating libraries is available in the Management file later this year, the Committee will be able to compare purchasing activities and collection use by the Conspectus structure used to assume primary or secondary collecting responsibility. The value of this information will, of course, increase as additional years of data are available, but I'm confident the initial report will be helpful for gaining a better understanding of the relation between each library and the group as a whole. Also, in view of the extensive survey of ILL and resource sharing just completed, a study charting the volume and patterns of ILL activity which indicated that monographs account for 75 percent of all ILLs in Alaska, adding the perspective of ILL by subject obtainable from the Management file will be of particular interest.

Another benefit of using the Management file was coming to appreciate fully the flexibility of the WLN Conspectus. When planning how to use the file for my library, I realized I needed Conspectus divisions for nonprint material and for fiction if the data was to reflect a public library collection accurately, and these additions were both simple and effective. This ability to add local divisions or specific lines to the Conspectus makes the software applicable for both single libraries and consortia. this flexibility is also built into the Management file, since it, too, can be used at any level, or combination of levels, as appropriate for the type or size of library and for the nature of the project.

FUTURE

A recognition of the Management file's power and flexibility has pointed to the next phase of the Conspectus project in Alaska: using the process to train even very small libraries in the techniques of conspectus-based collection management. Although few of them will ever have in-house access to the software, their data, most at the division level, can be added to the database and be used to help in both local and statewide planning activities and help develop a more extensive network of local cooperative agreements.

References

1. *Alaska Cooperative Collection Development Agreement*, (Anchorage: Anchorage Municipal Libraries, in progress), 1-2.
2. Paul H. Mosher, "Resource Sharing and Collection Development in Alaska: Distributed Interde-

pendence and the Future of Alaska," in *Alaska is a Library*, edited by Nancy Lesh and B. Jo Morse (Anchorage: University of Alaska Anchorage Library, 1984), 41.

3. Raymond McLeod, *Management Information Systems*, 3d ed. (Chicago: Science Research Associates, 1986), 17.

Bibliography

Alaska Cooperative Collection Development Agreement. Anchorage: Anchorage Municipal Libraries, in progress.

Ferguson, A.W. "The Conspectus and Cooperative Collection Development: What It Can and Cannot Do." *Acquisitions Librarian,* 4 (Number 7, 1992): 105-114.

Lesh, Nancy and B. Jo Morse, eds. *Alaska is a Library.* Anchorage: University of Alaska Anchorage Library, 1984.

Malyshev, Nina, ed. *Resource Sharing in Alaska: Report and Recommendations.* Fairbanks: Alaska Collection Development Steering Committee, 1993.

Pinnell-Stephens, June. "President's Foreword. After Assessment: Building on the Conspectus for Collection Management." *PNLA Quarterly,* 57 (Winter, 1993): 2+.

Powell, Nancy and Mary Bushing, *WLN Collection Assessment Manual,* 4th ed. Lacey, WA: WLN, 1992.

Stephens, Dennis. "Multi-type Library Collection Planning in Alaska: A Conspectus-Based Approach." *Acquisitions Librarian,* 4 (Number 7, 1992): 137-156.

APPENDIX A.

EDUCATION

Classification: LC: L-LT   DDC: 370-379
Conspectus: LC: EDU000   DDC: EDD000

	LIBRARY	LVL	COMM
HISTORY OF EDUCATION			
LC: LA	*AkAU 3a	2b	
Con: EDU 004.5-069	AkJU	2a	1b
DDC:	AkU	2b	1b
Con:			
THEORY & PRACTICE OF EDUCATION			
LC: LB	Ak	2a	2a
Con: 0069.5-112	*AkAU	3b	3a
DDC: 370.1-373, 375, 378	AkJU	2b	2b
Con: EDD101-049, 060, 090	AkPalU	1b	2a
	AkU	3b	2b

* Primary collecting library. All other listed are secondary collectors.

Scope notes on EDUCATION areas:

Ak: Collection includes ERIC and college catalog microfiche collections.

AkA: Emphasis on reading, storytelling, the gifted and early childhood education.

AkAU: Shelf list estimate 6200 vols. ERIC/college catalogs on microfiche.

AkF: Emphasis on directories. Have college catalog microfiche collection. Local responsibility for homeschooling.

AkJ: Depend heavily on Ak & AkJU, with exception of preschool, early childhood, home schooling, & college guides.

AkJU: Shelf estimate: 2300 vols. ERIC/College catalogs on microfiche.

AkU: Shelf estimate: 7100 vols. ERIC/College catalogs.

Note: Absence of current curriculum text collection statewide.

Fiction Assessment: An Introduction

by Georgine Olson, Issue Co-Editor

The development and use of a fiction assessment conspectus is explored in three article.

First, Shay Baker explores the general environment in which fiction col lections have been developed, addresses the seeming paradox of *demand* vs. *quality,* and suggests that using a fiction assessment tool would assist librarians by focusing their concepts of collection building and providing a map for the further development of their fiction collections.

Second, Burns Davis writes about Nebraska's library-driven search for a fiction assessment tool. The author shares the products and processes that were developed and explains how the Baker, WLN, and other tools fit into that project.

Third, Marietta Weber explains the rather far-reaching effect upon fiction collection management participation as a test site for the Baker project had in her small rural Illinois library.

Quality And Demand: The Basis For Fiction Collection Assessment

by Sharon L. Baker

Over the past half century, librarians have been increasingly interested in carefully and systematically examining their collections—making changes to strengthen and develop these sets of materials at both the individual library and the regional levels. Most of the techniques used to conduct these examinations were originally designed to evaluate the quality of nonfiction collections in academic libraries. In the past few decades, public librarians have successfully modified these techniques to evaluate both the quality and the use of their nonfiction collections. Recently, there has been surprisingly little literature on how these techniques could be applied directly to the evaluation of *fiction* collections in public libraries.[1]

This lack of material stems, at least in part, from the early days of the public library movement when some librarians with elitist tendencies suggested, often vehemently, that *factual works*—attempting as they do to discuss the reality, actuality, or truth of a situation—were somehow better than *fictitious works*—the imaginative, fanciful, or even "capricious" creations of an author. These librarians de-emphasized fiction access in the card catalog and used various tactics to try to wean patrons away from the frivolous reading of fiction. For example, proponents of the two-book system allowed patrons to check out two, rather than one, book at a time *if* the second was non-fiction.[2] Still other librarians placed fiction in a ribbon arrangement:

> . . . on one shelf around the room, with non-fic-

tion classes above and below it, the expectation being that many users who read only fiction (would) in this way be attracted to non-fiction books and begin to withdraw and read them.[3]

Although faint echoes of these elitist tactics are still infrequently heard, most have disappeared over time. Today, public librarians generally agree that works of fiction and of nonfiction share many important characteristics. Both can present information about past and present acts, events, people, places, and other objects. Both can speculate about the future. Both can contain information that enlightens our understanding of our history, surroundings, and motivations; enriches our ability to think creatively and solve problems successfully; entertains us with vivid descriptions and playful language; and evokes feelings of serenity or turmoil, joy or despair.

But while public librarians have accepted that fiction has an important place in their collections, there is evidence that controversy still remains over the variety and quantity of fiction of different types that should be included in public library collections, a controversy often referred to as "the quality versus demand debate."

This article briefly describes the philosophical underpinnings of this debate, noting that the debate, as it has been couched in the past, has actually muddied our understanding of the issue. The article also suggests a revised logical framework for understanding collection development in public libraries, a framework that was used to construct a fiction collection assessment tool for all sizes of libraries.

Sharon L. Baker is Associate Professor, University of Iowa School of Library and Information Science in Iowa City.

QUALITY VERSUS DEMAND: THE ERRONEOUS CONTINUUM

Advocates of the "quality" approach to collection development generally argue that public libraries are responsible for educating the citizens they serve by providing works of permanent value, elevating the cultural level of community residents, nurturing ideas, encouraging the development of a variety of diverse points of view, and preserving knowledge for future generations.[4] But critics say selectors who overemphasize quality can create elitist collections that are far above the tastes and needs of the average reader. They add that this selection bias has caused most public libraries to be used by a small segment of the total population, a segment that is predominantly white, middle-class, well-educated, and female.[5]

Those who advocate demand selection argue that even works of outstanding quality are not worth their cost if no one will read, view, or listen to them.[6] These libraries use a variety of techniques to systematically study customer needs, wants, and preferences, screening potential purchases by anticipated use *before* considering other selection criteria such as quality. Practices like these (and related strategies such as paying attention to the size of print runs, advertising budgets, and media exposure for specific titles) have led to accusations that demand-oriented libraries serve mainly middle-class popular fiction readers, equate circulation counts with the library's goals, surrender responsibility for book selection to publishers who are more interested in making profit than in promoting societal interests, and contribute to a general decline in collection quality.[7]

In short, we end up with a situation where accusations and epithets are hurled by both sides. Unfortunately, this situation is exacerbated by our habit of continually and erroneously referring to this issue as "the quality *versus* demand debate." "Versus" in this context implies that "quality" and "demand" are mutually exclusive aspects of library materials—dichotomous or (at the least) located at opposite ends of the same continuum. The reality is, however, that "quality" and "demand" represent two separate dimensions of any given work.

RENAMING THE DEBATE: QUALITY *AND* DEMAND

We can illustrate this convergence logically by examining several definitions. First, a dichotomy literally means a group that is split asunder into two sharply distinguished, opposed, or contrasting categories. Division into a dichotomy assumes that a class of objects can be clearly defined and then separated into opposing sets. We could, for example, examine a list of 100 different answers to an English spelling test and then divide the responses into the dichotomous categories of "correct" and "incorrect." Such a division is easy when one is dealing with *objective* measures, such as facts or other easily defined or standardized information; information that can be checked for accuracy in any number of standard reference sources.

It is possible, of course, to define the terms "quality" and "demand" in such a way that they too are objective rather than subjective. For example, we could define a "quality" title as one that had received one of ten major literary awards during the last 50 years and a "demand" title as one that had sold at least 10,000 copies nationwide in the last two years. But doing so forces a gross oversimplification of characteristics that are much richer and more complex than these admittedly factual but very narrow definitions address.

Therefore, it makes sense to erase the notion of dichotomous, black-and-white thinking; replacing it with the more complex notion of a continuum, which considers many shades of gray. A continuum is an unbroken, connected line that represents a progression of values on the same dimension, moving from one extreme to another by minute degrees.

We need to be careful though about the labels we place at the end of each continuum, since we have erred in the past by locating quality at one end of a single continuum and demand at the other. Librarians who do this are faced with an impossible dilemma, one convincingly described in an often quoted editorial by John Berry, esteemed editor of *Library Journal*.

> You have to respond to public demand. When you base book selection and retention on circulation and demand, you bring objectivity to the problem. You can use the easier measures of circulation figures. . . No doubt about it, basing book selection on popular demand is easier, is measurable, is more objective.
>
> When you actually try to judge the books or make conscious selections, you risk subjectivity. You have to make those forbidden "value judgments." You risk buying books that won't be used. You can't always afford to supply enough copies of popular books . . .
>
> In truth, it is impossible and unrealistic to come down squarely on either side of the "demand vs. quality" debate. Every librarian knows that. It is one of the frustrating dilemmas of our professional practice.[8]

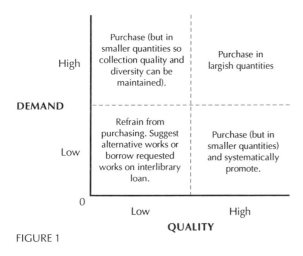

FIGURE 1

The graph shows DEMAND on the vertical axis (High and Low) and QUALITY on the horizontal axis (Low and High), with four quadrants:

- High Demand, Low Quality: Purchase (but in smaller quantities so collection quality and diversity can be maintained).
- High Demand, High Quality: Purchase in largish quantities
- Low Demand, Low Quality: Refrain from purchasing. Suggest alternative works or borrow requested works on interlibrary loan.
- Low Demand, High Quality: Purchase (but in smaller quantities) and systematically promote.

Berry's dilemma, and those of the rest of us who have considered this matter, is lessened greatly by the simple realization that quality and demand do not represent opposing ends of a single continuum. Rather, as Figure 1 shows, they represent two continuum that measure different aspects of the same work. That is, the categories of "quality" and "demand" are not mutually exclusive Works that are of high quality may also be those that have great demand (e.g., one on the bestseller list), may have lower but steady demand (e.g., a literary classic), or may have little demand (e.g., a novel by a previously unpublished author).

In fact, high quality and low quality works stand at opposite ends of a single continuum representing quality. Fiction titles that are highest in quality are those that challenge a reader's attitudes and beliefs, are written in a thoughtful and insightful fashion, use language imaginatively, address significant subjects, possess literary merit, feature complex characters; and/or have fascinating or intricate plots.[9] While not all quality titles possess all of these characteristics, works that consistently have more of these elements are generally thought to be of higher quality than works that have fewer.

Similarly, fictitious works that are not well known to the public for a variety of reasons lie at one end of the continuum representing demand. They may be written by a first-time or foreign author, cover a topic in which a limited number of people are interested, or use a specialized vocabulary that cannot be readily understood by a large number of people. Works that are in more demand may be classics or perennial favorites, may be those that have temporarily caught the public's interest and imagination, may be written by people who have built up a following over time, or may be diligently promoted by publishers.

The Four Quadrants of Collection Development

As Figure 1 shows, our selection practices can be more readily explained if we think of the four quadrants of the graph as representing different selection choices. Ideally, public librarians would try to purchase all titles that fall into the high demand, high quality quadrant in large quantities (the number purchased will, of course, vary by size of library), thereby meeting the needs of community residents who are asking for these titles and fulfilling the public library's objective of providing materials to educate, enlighten, and entertain its patrons.

Titles that lie in the high quality, low demand quadrant should also be purchased. However, to ensure cost-effectiveness in their collection development efforts, public librarians will want to buy fewer copies of each *and* systematically promote their use, via standard promotion techniques like book talks, book lists, book displays, and the like.

Public librarians will also purchase a number of items that patrons are requesting but that are not of the highest quality—e.g., series romance novels. However, librarians should buy fewer individual copies of these items to ensure that they will have enough money to purchase higher quality works and maintain a degree of collection diversity.

Finally, public librarians should generally refrain from purchasing titles that are low in quality and in demand, meeting patron needs by suggesting alternative sources of a higher quality or borrowing requested works for patrons on interlibrary loan.

Considering collection development in this way will allow us, as librarians, to use our creative talents "to build (fiction) collections that can lead readers to new discoveries and old truths, to a richer reading life, as often as it follows those readers down the path to popularity's familiar and safe tastes."[10]

It should also allow us to spend less time talking about "the quality versus demand" issue in a way that is divisive and more time conducting effective evaluations of our fiction collections.

The Philosophical Base for Fiction Collection Evaluation

The fiction collection assessment tool, first created for use by public libraries of various sizes in the Lincoln Trail and Corn Belt library systems in Illinois, is based on the philosophy that public libraries should consider both quality and demand when examining their collections. The assessment tool asks librarians to determine the overall quality of their collection by:

- examining the size and growth rate of the general fiction and genre fiction collections, looking at both diversity (examining the total number of authors and titles owned) and duplication levels (comparing the number of titles and volumes owned),
- determining from these figures the level of collection intensity in given areas (e.g., minimal level or comprehensive level), and
- checking library holdings against three specially compiled lists—of recent award winning titles, of classic fiction titles, and of ALA's notable titles.

The assessment tool also suggests that librarians should measure demand by:

- scrutinizing reserve lists to identify heavily used fiction,
- examining aggregate circulation records to determine classes of fiction that are heavily (or lightly) used,
- conducting availability studies to determine the extent to which patrons can find desired fiction titles when they are initially sought,
- checking library holdings against a specially compiled list of recent bestselling fiction, and
- identifying items that are desired but are not in the collection, through examination of interlibrary loan records, systematic solicitation of patron purchase suggestions, and focus group discussions.

It will not always be possible, of course, for a library to use each of the assessment procedures described in the fiction collection assessment tool. But, as the libraries who have used the tool have found, these evaluation techniques can reveal some surprising information about the quality and use of their fiction collections; information that will ideally be utilized to alter purchasing or overall collection management practices. The procedures can also, when used on a regional basis, allow systems of libraries to work cooperatively to enhance the strengths in their existing collections and correct any deficiencies found.

References

1. There are, of course, some notable exceptions. For example, when one researcher checked a list of 100 significant, older, in-print Canadian novels against the holdings of several types of agencies, he concluded that the public library is doing a much better job of providing access to literature for that member of the general public who is a serious reader than new bookstores and second-hand bookstores (who were limited by shelf space and by market demand in terms of what they were willing to carry) and academic library collections (who often restricted borrowing privileges of the general public in order to better meet the needs of the students and faculty they were mandated to serve). See Richard Hopkins, "Satisfying the Needs of the Serious Reader," *Canadian Library Journal* 44:81-84, 86-87 (April 1987).

2. Catherine Sheldrick Ross, "Readers' Advisory Services: New Directions," *RQ* 30:503-518 (Summer 1991).

3. Arthur E. Bostwick, *The American Public Library* (4th ed.; New York: Appleton, 1929), pp. 195-96.

4. See, for example, John Berry, "Leaning Toward Quality," *Library Journal* 115:76 (15 June 1990); Murray, Bob, "The Case for Quality Book Selection," *Library Journal* 107:1701-1710 (15 September 1982); and John P. Dessauer, "Are Libraries Failing Their Patrons?" *Publisher's Weekly* 2217:67-68 (18 January 1980).

5. See, for example, Carol Hole, "Click! The Feminization of the Public Library, " *American Libraries* 21:1076-1079 (December 1990); Barbara B. Moran, "Popular Culture and Library Education," *Journal of Education for Library and Information Science*, 26:25-32 (Summer 1985); Andrea C. Dragon and Tony Leisner, "The ABCs of Implementing Library Marketing," *Journal of Library Administration* 4:33-47 (Winter 1983); and Jane Hirsch, comment made during a panel discussion at Lancaster, Pennsylvania, on October 3, 1979—quoted in Judy Nyren, "Library Bookstore Syndrome Eyed in Lancaster," *Library Journal* 104:2512-2514 (1 December 1979).

6. Nora Rawlinson, "Give 'Em What They Want!" *Library Journal* 115:76 (15 June 1990).

7. Again, see Reference #4.

8. John Berry, "Leaning Toward Quality," *Library Journal* 115:76 (15 June 1990).

9. These aspects of quality novels have been described in a variety of collection development texts including those by Sharon L. Baker, *The Responsive Public Library Collection* (Englewood, CO: Libraries Unlimited, 1993); G. E. Gorman and B. R. Howes, *Collection Development for Libraries* (New York: Bowker-Saur, 1989); G. Edward Evans, *Developing Library and Information Center Collections* (2d. ed., Littleton, CO: Libraries Unlimited, 1987); Arthur Curley and Dorothy Broderick, *Building Library Collections* (6th. ed., Metuchen, NJ: Scarecrow Press, 1985); and Peter H. Mann, *Books: Buyers and Borrowers* (London: Deutsch, 1971).

10. John Berry, "Leaning Toward Quality," *Library Journal* 115:76 (15 June 1009).

Designing A Fiction Assessment Tool: The Customer Service Approach

by Burns Davis

Why create another collection assessment tool? One reason is the highly personal nature of the assessment process. Each local library describes and evaluates its own collection in relation to the library's goals for meeting the needs of its local clients. In our times of focusing on local needs, each library wants to customize the assessment process to meet local challenges as closely as possible. These local needs are greatly felt in the data collection step of the assessment process. An intermediate tool is helpful for collecting and organizing appropriate categories of data to prepare information for entry onto the WLN Conspectus worksheets and database, or into other assessment methods if desired.

Another reason for developing a new tool is that assessment of fiction materials is still in a process of refinement. Two of the most thoroughly structured methods have been developed for New Zealand[1] and the joint project of Corn Belt Library System and Lincoln Trail Libraries System in Illinois.[2] These tools have provided invaluable inspiration for working out a fiction assessment method and tool for Nebraska libraries. However, neither of these methods, nor any others that were examined, seemed to exactly match our need for a method that coordinated data preparation in small- and medium-sized libraries with the WLN Conspectus assessment methods and tools, yet remained relatively uncomplicated and self-determined.

Fiction materials are especially important to public library and school media center collec-tions. In Nebraska, public libraries desiring to achieve accreditation must meet a certain num-ber of collection development planning objec-tives. State guidelines for school media certification require collection assessment. Ideas for developing a fiction assessment tool came from the needs of these libraries to practice assessment techniques.

COMPARISON OF METHODS AVAILABLE

The first step in locating an appropriate fiction assessment tool for small libraries in Nebraska was to search for an existing tool and consider using it. Several possibilities were considered. The *Collection Profile, Acquisitions, Budget Man-ual* by Ruth Graham[3] in New Zealand offered a thorough, organized methodology compatible with the WLN Conspectus. This method provides an especially detailed approach for budget plan-ning and tracking. To suit the less centralized library community in our area, a less complex, less time-consuming method was sought for accomplishing well-organized data collection. The *Fiction Collection Assessment Manual* by Sharon Baker and Patricia Boze,[4] a product of the Corn Belt and Lincoln Trail project, produced a complete process especially for fiction materials which is coordinated with the WLN Conspectus. This method seems designed for use with a more formally organized library community than ours and incorporates complex data collection tech-niques, such as availability studies, which are more intensive than most Nebraska libraries were prepared to implement. Many of the ideas in

Burns Davis is Information Resources Coordinator at the Nebraska Library Commission. She has had training and experience in public and academic libraries. Her MLS is from the University of Oklahoma.

these two methods were helpful. The Fiction Collection Intensity Indicators from the *Fiction Collection Assessment Manual*[5] were used, by permission, because they are clearly written definitions that parallel the Collection Codes in the *WLN Collection Assessment Manual*.[6]

The WLN Conspectus provides the basic assessment methods and tools upon which our assessment process is based. At the time our fiction worksheet was developed, the WLN Conspectus was in version 4.15 which had not yet fully developed fiction assessment capabilities. Our fiction worksheet was designed to allow assessors to collect data for fiction materials that could be entered as a locally created division in the WLN Conspectus database. The Fiction Worksheet for Small Public Libraries developed by Nancy Powell, which was published in an earlier version of the conspectus manual,[7] provided an example of effective, simple worksheet design.

Personal experiences in small rural libraries and in branch libraries regarding collection management provided knowledge of the possibilities for collecting and evaluating entire collections, training staff who held a wide range of job classifications, and using results for decision making and supporting library budget needs. This experience was helpful for applying assessment techniques and tools in an automated format for small libraries.

All of these sources provided valuable ideas about ways of organizing and tabulating data, checkpoints of what is essential data to collect, experience in use of the collated results, checking for completeness of instructions, experience in time needed to obtain data and prepare reports, and knowledge about how to apportion the work and who could be trained to perform the various tasks. At this point, step-by-step directions and a design format that matched our existing nonfiction assessment data worksheets were needed.

THE GOAL

The goal was to find a simple way to organize data for assessing fiction materials using an uncomplicated data collection tool that would coordinate with the WLN Conspectus and provide data which could be used for plain-spoken reports relevant to local library decision making.

The Nebraska Library Commission has a continuing collection development commitment to provide consultation, develop methods and tools, and provide the statewide assessment database for collection development. The state planning guidelines for public libraries have components related to collection development. The certification program for librarians and the Basic Skills Training Program which are administered by the Library Commission also have collection development components. A primary objective of the collection management training and the collection analysis performed for the Library Commission's collection has been the development and trial of procedures and tools which can be used by small- and medium-sized libraries in assessing their own collections.

Comments from librarians throughout the state inspired the primary objectives for locating assessment methods and tools. Their message stated clearly that there was a need to make standard methodology available at low cost with accessible training *and* to promote use of collection assessment results to manage collections. They also wanted ways to make it possible for them to perform valid collection assessments without additional staff, expensive tools, or complicated techniques.

The Customer Service Approach: Focus on What Librarians Want

Discussion of probable assessment needs of Nebraska libraries with librarians in small libraries throughout the state delivered a very clear message that the assessment methods must be simple and fast. Since the librarians are the people for whom the fiction assessment tool is intended, the following "laundry list" of their specifications guided the worksheet design and assessment training:

1. Assessment methods must be flexible, individualized, and locally determined—allowing maximum independence for application of the standardized methodology.
2. Assessment methods should be descriptive of all types of materials and collection levels, and be applicable to all types of libraries.
3. Assessments must be manageable within one person's (or one small team's) regular working schedule.
4. Trainers should provide one source of instructions in a workbook or handbook.
5. Trainers should avoid jargon.
6. There should be low theory content in the training. Focus training on procedures—i.e., how to do it.
7. Training should be provided for using assessment results easily in budget planning and presentations.
8. Reports of assessment results must be reducible to one page, or at most, a few pages.
9. The Nebraska Library Commission must support the software applications: libraries should not have to perform spreadsheet or conspectus

data entry, but should have the option of obtaining the software on request.

10. The Nebraska Library Commission should provide assistance in setting up local interdisciplinary divisions in the conspectus data base.

Library Characteristics Influence Shape of Tool

Implementing collection assessment in Nebraska means addressing the needs of libraries for which size is an important consideration in planning. There are 1138 libraries in Nebraska, of which 652 are school libraries, 279 public, and the other 207 libraries are academic, institutional, special, and state resource libraries. Two public libraries serve populations over 50,000. Of all the public libraries in Nebraska, 89 percent serve rural areas; most of which are in areas that might be described as geographically isolated. Most libraries in Nebraska are in communities of under 20,000 people. Smaller still are the 238 public libraries that serve populations of 10,000 and under. Staff size is generally small. The majority of Nebraska libraries are staffed by one to 12 people.[8]

Thinking small is big. Nebraska library characteristics are representative of the majority of public libraries in the United States. Rural is defined by Bernard Vavrek, Coordinator of the Center for the Study of Rural Librarianship, as a place no larger than 25,000 residents, and not within a Metropolitan Statistical Area. Approximately 80 percent of the 15,312 public libraries in the U.S. serve populations located in nonmetropolitan areas.[9] With these facts in mind, it seemed reasonable to focus on the collection assessment needs of small libraries.

Assessment Tool Specifications

In deciding what design criteria to use, the minimum data collection techniques recommended by current collection assessment practices were matched with what was known about realistic work expectations and useful data for decision making models in small libraries. Based on these ideas, a data collection tool was sought that would be flexible, comprehensive, simple, and shareable. These characteristics were met by using the following criteria to guide the design of the fiction assessment worksheet.

1. Flexible
A. Use spread sheet software for formatting in order to speed up calculation of data totals and percentages. Spread sheet format can also be used to prepare projections.
B. Design format for collecting observations during shelf scanning as well as for entering tabu-

lated shelflist counts and other counts.
C. Design format to collect data in a form useful to libraries entering their own data in the WLN Conspectus file as well as libraries sending in their data to Nebraska Library Commission for entry.
D. Design format to contain spaces for basic assessment data, but permit adaptation for libraries planning to collect more types of data. Allow data collection at the broadest level as well as at the most specific level.
E. Design format to contain elements for collecting data useful for management information reports that can now be generated from the WLN Conspectus Management Information File.
F. Design tools for use by both LC- and Dewey-classified libraries.

2. Comprehensive
A. Show use-oriented data as well as collection-oriented data on the worksheet.
B. Correlate data for all information resource formats to WLN conspectus categories in the worksheet.
C. Provide the capability for assessing all reading audiences (levels) and genres.

3. Simple
A. Keep worksheets to the minimum number necessary for collecting adequate data for a complete assessment.
B. Keep types of data collected to the minimum amount necessary for completing an adequate assessment.
C. Design the worksheet for use with minimum training by a wide variety of job positions during data collection and data entry.

4. Shareable
A. Coordinate the fiction worksheet with other data collection tools offered and used by the Nebraska Library Commission.
   • Median Age Tally Sheet (Figure 1)
   • Dewey-Based Assessment Data Worksheet
   • LC-Based Assessment Data Worksheet
   • Assessment Data Worksheet Summary (Figure 3)
   • WLN Conspectus Database Worksheets
B. Make the product available in photo-ready or diskette format.
C. Design the worksheet to be appropriate for use in libraries of all sizes.
D. Design results to be shareable in WLN comparison reports with other small libraries regardless of type.

FORMATTING THE CONSPECTUS

The least number of forms possible was desired because a small number of forms is less confusing to coordinate, and it is easier to visualize data and refer between small numbers of forms. Types

MEDIAN AGE TALLY SHEET -- NONFICTION/FICTION

DIVISION_____

GENRE (Adventure, Romance, etc.)_____

Use this form to enter information about individual items examined from the collection during shelf scanning.

Enter tally marks under category on the appropriate date line.

Total: add the number of tally marks for all years in each category.

Median Age: count down to half the total tally marks in the category. Enter the year.

Observe physical condition

Year of Publication	TOTAL	CATEGORY or FORMAT (hard cover, large print, etc.)						
		ADULT	YA	JUVENILE	EASY READERS	PICTURE BOOKS	LARGE PRINT	SPECIAL COLLECTIONS
1994								
1993								
1992								
1991								
1990								
1989								
1988								
1987								
1986								
1980-85								
1975-79								
1970-74								
1960s								
1950s								
pre 1950								
TOTAL								
MEDIAN AGE								
Physical Condition								
Notes								

FIGURE 1

of data that could be expressed in the fewest words possible or expressed numerically were selected. There was a preference to avoid duplicating other methods and, at the same time, represent current theory and methods of collection assessment and library management. There was also an effort to reduce instructions to a few pages at most and a one-day assessment training.

The worksheet and assessment methods were to be compatible with the WLN Conspectus worksheets. It was desirable that the data flow in sequence from one worksheet to another during the processes of data collection; resulting in completion of the WLN Conspectus worksheet and entry into the database (or into the library's assessment report if the librarian chose not to use the WLN Conspectus).

It was also desirable to build on the experience acquired through the Nebraska Library Commission assessment. In that process we had developed tried and usable data collection methods and tools suitable for small libraries. The nonfiction worksheets were tested in use during the Nebraska Library Commission assessment and handled the data flow in the desired manner. Therefore, the fiction data worksheet was based on the nonfiction worksheets and incorporated into the training and the *Collection Assessment Manual for Small- and Medium-Sized Libraries.*[10]

An effort was made to fulfill what the librarians wanted and to accommodate the needs of small libraries as much as possible. The resulting Fiction Assessment Data Worksheet is shown in Figure 2. The final product is formatted to collect the minimum necessary qualitative and quantitative data. The design focused on the most easily-collected, fastest-tallied, simply-measured, and easily-understood elements recognized as significant data by library management in current practice.

Paraprofessional and clerical staff participated in the worksheet development by checking for clarity of layout and meaning of terms. This was an important contribution because staff in a wide variety of job classifications will perform much of the data collection in many libraries. Volunteers may collect data in some libraries. During the Nebraska Library Commission assessment, the worksheets for nonfiction materials were tried and found useable for a small library. The worksheets performed well for preparing data for entry onto WLN conspectus worksheets.

The fiction data worksheets present a data "picture" by categories of genre. By reviewing information that is entered on the assessment worksheet, staff can make informed decisions about assigning collection levels for conspectus categories and can prepare explicit comments relating to necessary collection management actions such as weeding, for example. Staff can also form descriptive comments about any outstanding characteristics of the materials in the category. Detailed acquisitions and use information data is also collected on the worksheet for entry into the conspectus management file.

Because the fiction worksheet coordinates with the nonfiction worksheet, it is possible to present a spreadsheet summary of the entire collection on the Assessment Data Worksheet Summary (see Figure 3). Since the worksheets are organized by the WLN Conspectus categories rather than being related to a classification schedule, the assessment data summary presents a picture of the entire collection of information resources for the library which is easily related to the WLN Conspectus reports. The summary format is useful background information for preparing brief presentations to library boards or funding bodies.

The Fiction Assessment Data Worksheet (see Figure 2) is formatted in Excel, version 4.0. Simple addition formulae result in column totals for collection-oriented and for use-oriented data elements. The percentage of total collection is automatically calculated for each genre and format. Reading levels are added on the Median Age Tally Sheet (see Figure 1). Data collectors can either enter numerical data and descriptive notes by hand on the worksheet and enter the data later into the Excel file; or they can enter data and notes directly into the Excel file on a laptop computer during shelf scanning and other data collection processes. The fiction worksheet was developed prior to the release of the current WLN Conspectus, version 5.0. A preliminary check shows the fiction worksheet to be compatible with the new version of the Conspectus. The fiction worksheet will be reformatted, where necessary, to correspond to the new fiction divisions of the WLN Conspectus. The underlying concept and types of data collected on the fiction worksheet will still be valid.

All data collection worksheets are based on the objective to obtain the minimum number of data types needed to complete an assessment. However, the data is collected and reported in such a way that it can be used with additional analysis techniques such as fill rate determination, availability surveys, or user satisfaction surveys. Representing qualitative and quantitative data is intended to lead to a thoughtful analysis that encourages the exercise of the librarian's professional knowledge and judgment. Because the worksheets are formatted as spreadsheets in Excel, librarians can massage the data into a variety of reports and set up predictive scenarios

FICTION ASSESSMENT DATA WORKSHEET

GENRE	Conspectus line number	Collection-Oriented Data													Use-Oriented Data					Recommended Action
		# volumes	% total collection	# titles	# authors	median age	# of volumes examined on shelf	# books-on-tape	#videotapes	# multimedia, electronic information sources	# hard cover	# paper-backs	# large print	NOTES: physical condition, language, weaknesses, strengths, uneven collecting	# ILL loaned	# ILL borrowed	Circulation	Reserves, requests	acquisitions in last year #/$	weeding, preservation, purchasing, etc.
(Source of data)	(WLN Conspectus)	(shelflist)	(shelflist)	(shelflist)	(shelflist)	(shelf observation every 5th volume)	(shelf observation every 5th volume)	(shelflist)	(shelflist)	(shelf observation)	(shelflist)	(shelflist)	(shelflist)	(shelf observation every 5th volume)	(system report)	(system report)	(system report)	(patron suggestions)	(system report)	(evaluator's opinion)
Adventure																				
General fiction																				
Mystery																				
Romance																				
Science fiction																				
Fantasy																				
Classic fiction																				
Biographical fiction																				

FICTION ASSESSMENT DATA WORKSHEET

Horror																						
Western																						
Historical fiction																						
Short stories																						
Other																						
TOTAL																						

FIGURE 2

Assessment Data Worksheet Summary

DIVISION/Category	Dewey Class	Conspectus line number	Collection-Oriented Data								Use-Oriented Data					Recommended Action
			# titles in collection	% total collection	median age	# of volumes examined on shelf	# journal titles owned	# audio/video titles owned	electronic information sources	Notes: uncataloged collections, physical condition, weaknesses/strengths, weeding needed, preservation factors	# ILL loaned	# ILL borrowed	Circulation	Reference questions answered/ Reserves	acquisitions in last year #/$	weeding, preservation, purchasing, etc.
(Source of data)	(class correlation tables)	(WLN Conspectus)	(shelflist)	(shelflist)	(shelf observation every 5th volume)	(shelf observation every 5th volume)	(library periodical holdings list)	(shelflist)	(shelf observation)	(observation)	(system report)	(system report)	(system report)	(ref.sample/ patron sug.)	(system report)	(evaluator's opinion)
AGRICULTURE	630-639,712	AGO000														
ANTHROPOLOGY	306, 390-395, 398-399, 572-573	ANO000														
ART AND ARCHITECTURE	069, 700-711, 720-779	ARO000														
BIOLOGICAL SCIENCES	570,574-599	BIO000														
BUSINESS AND ECONOMICS	310, 314-319, 330-339, 368, 380-388, 650-653, 657-659	BUD000														
CHEMISTRY	540-548	CHD000														
COMPUTER SCIENCE	003-006, 621.39	CSO000														
EDUCATION	370-379	EDO000														
ENGINEERING AND TECHNOLOGY	527,600, 620-625, 627-629, 640-648, 660-688, 690-698	END000														
GEOGRAPHY AND EARTH SCIENCES	526, 549-560, 910-919	GEO000														
HISTORY AND AUXILIARY SCIENCES	900-998	HID000														
LANGUAGE, LINGUISTICS, AND LITERATURE	400-499	LAD000														
LAW	340-349	DLA000														
LIBRARY SCIENCE, GENERALITIES AND REFERENCE	000-002, 010-028, 030, 050-099	DL5000														
MATHEMATICS	510-516,519	MAD000														
MEDICINE	610-619	DME000														
MUSIC	780-789	MUD000														
PERFORMING ARTS	790.2, 791-792, 793.3, 793.8	PED000														
PHILOSOPHY AND RELIGION	100-129, 140-149, 160-199, 200-299	PHD000														
PHYSICAL EDUCATION AND RECREATION	372.86, 613.7, 790, 793-799	DPH000														

PHYSICAL SCIENCES	389, 500-509, 520-523, 525, 528-539	PUD000
POLITICAL SCIENCE	320-325, 327-328, 350-359	POD000
PSYCHOLOGY	130, 150, 152-156, 158	PSD000
SOCIOLOGY	300-305, 307, 326, 360-367, 649	SOD000
TOTAL NON-FICTION COLLECTION		
TOTAL FICTION COLLECTION	(reserves)	
TOTAL COLLECTION		

	Collection-Oriented Data									Use-Oriented Data					Recommended Action
DIVISION/Category	Conspectus line number	# titles in collection	% total collection	median age	# of volumes examined on shelf	# journal titles owned	# audio/video titles owned	electronic information sources	Notes: uncataloged collections, physical condition, weaknesses/strengths, weeding needed, preservation factors	# ILL loaned	# ILL borrowed	Circulation	Reference questions answered/ Reserves	acquisitions in last year #/$	weeding, preservation, purchasing, etc.
(Source of data)	(WLN Conspectus)	(shelflist)	(shelflist)	(shelf observation every 5th volume)	(shelf observation every 5th volume)	(library periodical holdings list)	(shelflist)	(shelf observation)	(observation)	(system report)	(system report)	(system report)	(ref.sample/ patron sug.)	(system report)	(evaluator's opinion)
ADULT															
YA															
JUVENILE															
EASY READERS															
PICTURE BOOKS															
LARGE PRINT															
SPECIAL COLLECTIONS															
TOTAL															

FIGURE 3

according to the needs of individual libraries.

DATA COLLECTION

Detailed explanations of fiction assessment theories can be located in other sources. Using the fiction assessment worksheet discussed in this article benefits librarians by informing them of:

1. the median age of a collection by formats, reading level, and category
2. budgeting
3. weeding and selecting
4. decisions about priorities
5. how library collection relate to public needs and service priorities
6. allocation/reallocation practices among branch libraries
7. cooperative collection development and resource sharing

The Fiction Assessment Worksheet is intended to be used with the *Collection Assessment Manual for Small- and Medium-Sized Libraries*[11] produced at the Nebraska Library Commission and with the *WLN Collection Assessment Manual.*[12]

In the *Collection Assessment Manual for Small- and Medium-Sized Libraries,*[13] assessors are instructed, step-by-step, through the general data collection process in order to create a collection profile. A library will need five types of worksheets to prepare for an assessment of the complete collection. The set of data worksheets for a Dewey- or LC-classified library collection contains:

- Median Age Tally Sheet (Figure 1)
- Fiction Assessment Data Worksheet (Figure 2)
- Assessment Data Worksheet Summary (Figure 3)
- WLN Conspectus Database Worksheets

To assess fiction as a distinctive division of the collection, information about the library's fiction collection is entered on the Fiction Assessment Data Worksheet (Figure 4) and on the WLN Fiction Conspectus Worksheets. The conspectus reports will separate fiction from nonfiction. Fiction may also be included in the overall assessment of information resources instead of treating fiction as a separate conspectus division.

Assessors are instructed to describe and evaluate their fiction resources using shelf observation and tabulation techniques using both use-oriented and collection-oriented data. They are then instructed to carry forward that information to a data summary about the total collection of information resources. Finally, assessors are instructed to enter data into the WLN Conspectus worksheets.

Assessors are given specific instructions for each data collection step. Data collection follows four general processes that proceeds from the collection of quantitative and qualitative data to the final entry into the WLN database. The following list is provided for assessors as a summary of the general steps in data collection.[14]

1. Collect and record data on the Median Age Tally Sheet (Figure 1), Dewey-Based Assessment Data Worksheet, and Fiction Assessment Data Worksheet (Figure 2) following the steps for qualitative data and quantitative data. Information about fiction assessment, reading levels, formats, special collections, and preservation is found in the WLN Conspectus Manual.[15]
2. Collate information from the Dewey-Based Assessment Data Worksheet and the Fiction Assessment Data Worksheet (Figure 2) by divisions on the Assessment Data Worksheet Summary (Figure 3).
3. Complete the WLN Conspectus Worksheet following instructions in the manual.[16]
4. When the data collection is completed, the assessors are to return their completed worksheets the library's Project Coordinator. The WLN worksheets or a conspectus diskette is sent to Nebraska Library Commission for entry into the WLN Conspectus database.

Instructions are provided which explain the various types of quantitative and qualitative data and guide assessors, step-by-step, through collecting and recording the data on the worksheets. The detailed instructions for recording data are located in the "Data Recording" section of this article.

DATA CATEGORIES

Many libraries group their fiction collection into categories for the convenience of their patrons. The categories used on the Fiction Data Assessment Worksheet (Figure 2) correspond, in general, to the categories used in the WLN Conspectus version 5.0. A category for multimedia (electronic information sources) was added on our worksheet. Information collected about formats, reading levels, and genres is entered on the Median Age Tally Sheet (Figure 1) and the Fiction Data Assessment Worksheet (Figure 2). The data categories assessed and recorded on the worksheets are listed below.

Genre:
- Adventure
- Biographical fiction
- General fiction
- Horror fiction

- Mystery
- Western fiction
- Romance
- Historical fiction
- Science fiction
- Short stories
- Fantasy
- Other
- Classic fiction

Format:
- Hardcover book
- Paperback book
- Large print book
- Videotape
- Books-on-tape
- Electronic Information Sources (Multimedia)

Reading Level:
- Adult
- Young Adult
- Juvenile
- Easy Readers
- Picture books

Information about fiction materials holdings is entered on the Fiction Assessment Data Worksheet (Figure 2) and on the Assessment Data Worksheet Summary (Figure 3) in the appropriate conspectus category. The holdings information may be incorporated in the comments column of the Conspectus Worksheets.

Libraries are encouraged to incorporate all information formats used by the library in their collection assessment. The format information may be entered at the subject level in the appropriate division of the WLN Fiction Conspectus Worksheets, or the library may choose to treat significant collections of materials formats, such as large print or videos, as interdisciplinary divisions of the conspectus.

RECORDING DATA

The instructions for collecting data are organized by quantitative and qualitative data. On the worksheet data is represented two-dimensional-

ly. The following grid shows the collection-oriented and use-oriented data that are collected for each genre. The local library would decide whether to use worksheets for each reading level or to use a combined worksheet for the entire fiction collection.

These are not exclusive categories, for instance, some user data can be considered to have both quantitative and qualitative characteristics; but thinking of the data in this way serves as a helpful reminder that observation and counting are both necessary steps to the assessment process. The instructions, as they are provided to the assessors in the *Assessment Manual for Small- and Medium-Sized Libraries,* are shown below.[17]

Quantitative Data

1. Using computer files or shelf list, ascertain the number of titles in the collection. Count electronic information sources (databases), non-book materials, serials, and periodical subscriptions. For fiction assessment, also count volumes and authors. Record this information on the Assessment Data Worksheets. Calculate the percentage of total holdings in each division/category/subject.
2. Determine expenditures in dollars and numbers of titles acquired during the year. Record this information on the Assessment Data Worksheet as acquisitions.
3. Collect information about circulation, interlibrary lending, and interlibrary borrowing. You may use a sample period if you do not have annual transaction information available. Try to select a time period that will yield at least 100 transactions. Record the number of circulations and interlibrary transactions in the appropriate conspectus categories on the Assessment Data Worksheets.
4. Collect information about reference questions. Use a sample period that will yield at least 100 questions. During the sample period, keep track of call numbers or database names of sources used to answer reference questions. Record the number of reference questions answered in the appropriate conspectus categories on the Assessment Data Worksheets.

TABLE 1

ASSESSMENT	QUANTITATIVE DATA	QUALITATIVE DATA
collection-centered	size of collection median age	expert (you) evaluation/shelf scan outside subject specialist evaluation
client-centered	use: ILL, reference circulation	user surveys community analysis

Qualitative Data

5. Obtain Shelf Observation data. This observation must be performed by a qualified expert: YOU. Go to the shelves with data collection sheets, the shelf list, and the Collection Development Policy and Selection Guidelines. Collect only data that will help make collection assessment decisions. Keep in mind that you are assessing the entire resource collection of information in all formats.

6. Examine every tenth book in collections which have 200 or more books per category. Examine every fifth book in collections which have fewer books per category. Examine every book in categories where there are fewer than five books.

7. Observe for each item examined:
   • date of publication
   • physical condition
   • appropriateness of subject coverage.
   Record the number of volumes examined on the shelf in that category.

8. Record date of publication on the Median Age Tally Sheet and calculate Median Age. Record the median age for the categories and division on the Assessment Data Worksheet.

9. Record observations about general physical condition and appropriateness of subject coverage on the Median Age Tally Sheet.

10. Summarize your observations about collection strengths, weeding needed, preservation status, acquisitions concerns, etc. Record these notes on the Assessment Data Worksheet. List checking is recommended only as a secondary method. It applies mostly to juvenile reading level materials. It is too time consuming for general assessment use. It is more useful in censorship issues, or selection and weeding decision making.

Complete the data recording for each category before moving to the next. Add relevant notes on the Assessment Data Worksheets for the category keeping in mind the following questions:

- What is the preservation status of materials in this category?
- Are the resources in this category heavily used for answering reference questions or filling requests?
- How many interlibrary loans lent/borrowed for this category?
- What is the coverage by state and federal documents, vertical file, indexes, electronic formats, periodicals?
- What are the current circulation and acquisition activities in this category?
- How do the available resources compare to the extent of information generally available in this field?

- How do our resources compare to our needs?
- Does this category need significant updating or weeding?

Fiction and nonfiction assessment data worksheets must be used with the median age tally sheet if collecting information by reading level is desired.

RESULTS

Several benefits are expected from use of the Fiction Assessment Data Worksheet (Figure 2) to organize data in preparation for entry onto the WLN conspectus worksheets. Training and communication about assessment methods and results are facilitated if one standardized method is the common ground. The worksheet format provides for collecting, describing, and evaluating the fiction resources in matrices of genre, format, and reading level. The matrix format encourages visualization of the dynamics of the relationships of a variety of characteristics in the collection as a whole. In this manner, the visualization process is maintained throughout the data collection phase of assessment, even before data is recorded on the WLN conspectus worksheets. Organized data can be reviewed at any point in the data collection process.

The data tabulated on the worksheet can be used in budget planning, determining resource sharing commitments, developing collection management action plans, allocating staff collection development responsibilities, and measuring progress on action plans even in those libraries which have stated a preference not to use the WLN Conspectus.

Inclusion of a data column for recommended actions encourages assessors to state an action plan for each category. Those action plans become part of the assessment and can be forwarded onto the WLN Conspectus worksheets.

Use of the fiction assessment data worksheets will allow libraries to collect and share information for cooperative collection development purposes in a common language regardless of classification scheme or library type. Libraries may elect not to use the WLN Conspectus, but will still be able to communicate in a common assessment terminology if they use these data collection worksheets. The data collection worksheets also would enable libraries limited to manual data collection to obtain information useful for collection management. Although use of the WLN Conspectus is encouraged, there is a necessity to avoid excluding choice by individual, local libraries.

THE FUTURE: NEBRASKA

Providing easily adapted tools and training is intended to encourage libraries of all sizes to methodically describe and evaluate their collections. The present objective is to encourage application of the assessment process in regular programs of collection management in Nebraska libraries. The next step is for Nebraska libraries to perform assessment; including fiction assessment. This will contribute to statewide cooperative collection development by facilitating common measurement of collection strengths and commitments.

Using the data collection tools will also make it possible for small libraries to obtain assessment results that can leverage their budgeting and bargaining power. Providing effective tools to collect detailed information about the make up and use of their collections may enable small libraries to engage in strategic targeting of resources. They will also be able to take advantage of comparative information about the collection over time. These benefits have been perceived in the past as mostly belonging to larger libraries, but the continuing improvement of assessment tools and simplified methods will bring these benefits to small libraries.

Dissemination of the fiction worksheets will be achieved by presenting training at the Nebraska Library Commission, at state association conferences, and during on-site library training. Wider offering of training will also be achieved through the basic skills units of continuing education for library staff throughout the state. It may also be productive to achieve greater communication with educational service districts; and to participate in statewide discussion among systems, boards, and the Nebraska Library Commission Advisory Council. Copies of the worksheet are available in print or 3.5" DOS compatible diskette to interested librarians.

FURTHER DEVELOPMENT

Assessment experience will lead to improvements in the instructions in the *Collection Assessment Manual for Small- and Medium-Sized Libraries*[18] and in the tool design. The worksheet format will be updated to coordinate with version 5.0 of the WLN Conspectus which now includes fiction assessment divisions. The worksheets will also be expanded to the WLN Conspectus subject level. The worksheets currently represent only the library science conspectus division at the subject level. All other divisions present data at the category level.

In implementing use of the WLN Conspectus Management Information File at the Nebraska Library Commission, trial use of fiction assessment information will be included in order to develop ways to make the file accessible for small libraries participating in the statewide database. Use of a laptop computer to directly enter data while assessors are shelf scanning will be tried as a way to increase the efficiency of data collection.

To explore where no assessors have gone before is the reward for librarians working with assessment tools. New applications will suggest themselves as local libraries present challenging needs. Suggestions from librarians will be encouraged and sought in order to find ways to improve and creatively utilize the data collection tools for small libraries.

References

1. Ruth Graham, *Collection Profile, Acquisitions, Budget Manual* (North Shore City, New Zealand: North Shore Libraries, 1992).
2. Sharon L. Baker, *Fiction Collection Assessment Manual*. Patricia J. Boze, ed. (Champaign, IL: Lincoln Trail Libraries System, 1992).
3. Graham.
4. Baker.
5. Ibid., 19.
6. Nancy Powell and Mary Bushing, *WLN Collection Assessment Manual*, 4th ed. (Lacey, WA: WLN, 1992).
7. Nancy Powell, ed., *Pacific Northwest Collection Assessment Manual*, 3d ed. (Salem, OR: The Pacific NW Collection Development Program, Oregon State Library Foundation, 1990), 58.
8. *Nebraska Public Library Profile: 1990-1991 Statistical Data* (Lincoln, NE: Nebraska Library Commission, 1992).
9. Bernard Vavrek, *Assessing the Information Needs of Rural Americans* (Clarion, PA: College of Library Science, Clarion University of Pennsylvania, 1990), 4-6.
10. Burns Davis, *Collection Assessment Manual for Small- and Medium-Sized Libraries*, (Lincoln, NE: Nebraska Library Commission, 1993).
11. Ibid.
12. Powell and Bushing.
13. Davis.
14. Ibid., 13-16.
15. Powell and Bushing.
16. Davis, 30.
17. Ibid., 15-16.
18. Ibid.

Bibliography

Baker, Sharon L. *Fiction Collection Assessment Manual*. Patricia J. Boze, ed. Champaign, IL: Lincoln Trail Libraries System, 1992.

Davis, Burns. *Collection Assessment Manual for Small- and Medium-Sized Libraries.* Lincoln, NE: Nebraska Library Commission, 1993.

Graham, Ruth. *Collection Profile, Acquisitions, Budget Manual.* North Shore City, New Zealand: North Shore Libraries, 1992.

Powell, Nancy and Mary Bushing. *WLN Collection Assessment Manual.* 4th ed. Lacey, WA: WLN, 1992.

Effects Of Fiction Assessment On A Rural Public Library

by Marietta Weber

The Chatsworth Township Library is located in the small Central Illinois village of Chatsworth. It has a total yearly budget under $20,000 and a population of 1,444 (1993). The library's primary role, established by a Citizens Survey, is to serve as a popular reading library for all ages. These were established facts when I became the librarian there in 1989. What's more, the Board of Trustees was concerned about the low circulation figures and wanted to generate more interest in library usage.

Why did I become interested in the Fiction Assessment Grant? Small libraries sometimes are subject to a rapid turnover in librarians—and this was the case at Chatsworth Township. Prior to 1989, there had been five librarians in nine years. My previous experience included six months as an assistant librarian and several years as an elementary school teacher. In the course of learning the necessary responsibilities required of a "one librarian library", I relied on the advice of the staff and workshops of our regional library system, Corn Belt Library System (CBLS). There were no guidelines for selecting material other than the best sellers for adults. While presenting the summer reading program and storyhours, I realized that we had few of the quality books needed for correlation with the summer reading program theme, so I found myself relying heavily on Easy Picture Book bulk loans from CBLS because our budget did not allow for the purchase of many new children's books.

When CBLS and Lincoln Trail Libraries System offered the opportunity of joining a group of small libraries in a Library Services and Construction Act (LSCA) grant proposal for a fiction cooperative collection management (CCM) project, I encouraged the Library Trustees to apply. I felt this would enable me to learn how to evaluate our fiction collection (something about which I had no experience or knowledge about). This might afford the library the opportunity to expand our collection without increasing our materials budget.

FICTION ASSESSMENT PROJECT

Getting to know your possible partners in a CCM project is very important. The travel and time away from the library are drawbacks, but the information gleaned is well worth the effort. The meetings among participating librarians were a great learning experience because ten librarians met at different libraries and shared information about the way their libraries worked.

The first goal of this project was to develop an assessment tool for fiction materials for public libraries. In order to develop the assessment tool, the project coordinators needed to know how small libraries were physically arranged, the budget of each, the process each used to access material into the library, and how and what records were kept for accession and circulation. To begin with, we learned how each library separated the standard fiction subdivisions in its shelflist and physical shelving. Examples of various ways to arrange fiction collections were discussed. Some are listed below: (table reference)

Chatsworth generally organizes its collection according to the reading level of the material. The physical arrangement and shelving of the

Marietta Weber is the Librarian at Chatsworth Township Public Library in Illinois.

TABLE 1

Fiction Genres:	
General fiction	Horror fiction
Mystery fiction	Western fiction
Romance fiction	Adventure fiction
Science fiction	Historical fiction
Fantasy fiction	Short Stories

Reading Levels:	
Adult	Picture Book
Young Adult	Easy Reader
Juvenile	

Formats:	
Hardback book	Videotape
Paperback book	Books-on-tape
Large print book	

collection is also guided by reading level. Shelves and shelf list are divided into these sections: Adult (hardback and paperback); Young Adult (hardback and paperback); Juvenile (hardback and paperback); Picture Books and Easy Reader (combined, including oversize and book/cassette kits).

As a result of these discussions and knowing what would be required of us for reporting later data, our library changed from a very simple daily circulation report form to a more complicated one which included a breakdown of nonfiction books checked out and also a breakdown of the different fiction genre within the reading levels. Later these statistics would be used in evaluating reader's choices and as a guide for ordering material. The information from these circulation reports were used in the library's Annual Reports and Illinois State Per Capita Grant application. It should be noted that we hand tally the circulation at Chatsworth, and the staff did not like the longer form at first. However, once they became familiar with the format and realized what valuable information it provided, they responded positively.

It had been mentioned by the project coordinators that spine labeling of books and even separate shelving of genre would enhance circulation. Therefore, we immediately ordered a more complete assortment of spine labels and began spine labeling by genre. At the same time we marked each circulation card with a letter symbol for the spine label (for example, R = romance). To help us decide what genre label to use for a particular title, we purchased *Genreflecting: A Guide to Reading Interests in Genre Fiction* by Betty Rosenberg and *A Handbook of Contemporary Fiction* by Mary K. Biagini. These

have proved to be invaluable sources for us as we "read shelves." In 1992, we grouped the adult hardback fiction genre of mystery and romance in separate shelf sections and have had positive patron response.

As part of the development of the assessment tool during the fiction grant project, each library had a specific area to test in addition to an area tested by all participating libraries.

Testing the size and depth of the collection measurement tool was required of all participating libraries. The plan included taking a sampling of the shelf list drawers. Specific instructions were given for measuring, counting, and recording the card statistics. Size of the collection would determine the time needed to do this measurement. This was done entirely by staff and did not take an excessive amount of time since our collection totals out at approximately 8500 volumes. Our results showed that we did not have great diversity in our collection but we felt this was not unusual since a popular reading library's patrons normally prefer reading a large number of the same author's works especially in adult fiction.

Chatsworth's specific task was to test "Growth Rate of Collection." This was not difficult because we began placing material purchases and deaccessions on a computer database as early as 1990. The staff and I find it easier to group and report on the various reading levels this way. When a library has one librarian and two assistants who usually work alone so the library can be open more hours and days of the week, computer databases are one way to always have information readily at hand. We also cross checked our results with our accession books. Our results were interesting because they showed a negative growth rate. This was due to the fact that we were in the midst of correcting our shelf list and bringing it up to date. Apparently, a large weeding project several years before had not been completed, and the shelf list cards had not been properly pulled and canceled. Also, no inventory of the collection had been done in the previous five or six years.

Since I had the help of a very competent Job Training Partnership Act student worker (JTPA is funded through the Illinois Department of Commerce and Community Affairs) at that time and I was very curious to see how our holdings rated against another project task, the check lists of Award Winners, Bestsellers, Classics, and ALA Notables, we also completed the assessment in these areas. The results were very enlightening! We found that the collection fell short in many of the areas especially in the children's materials. We also found that although, in a planning and role setting program, we had stated our primary goal was to be a popular reading library, the collection had been assessed according to the compiled list and found wanting! We determined that much more attention must be given to current best seller listings and published listings of quality material—especially in the area of children's material. At that time, the Board of Trustees made a commitment to concentrate on the children's collection in an effort to upgrade the quality of material purchased.

To me, rating the library's collection against these check lists was the most valuable tool in the assessment. The negative side of this evaluation is that the list is quickly dated. Small rural librarians do not have the staff time available to do the research needed to compile these lists. Using lists already given in published works (suggested by Corn Belt system staff) and loaned from the system collection were a great help when I again evaluated my children's collection prior to applying for the CBLS Deaccession Grant in 1991.

FICTION CCM PROJECTS

In the late fall of 1991, CBLS began their Deaccession CCM Grant Project. Headquarters planned to deaccess all materials except large print and library resources. Any system library forming a CCM program with other member libraries which was approved by the system would be allowed to have first choice of materials being deaccessed from the system headquarters collection. Each participating library would have to match, with local funds, the number of volumes (over a certain time period) that the system awarded to the library. Even though the fiction assessment results from comparing Chatsworth's holdings against the Check List of ALA notables, Award winners, etc. showed our inadequacy in those areas, it was apparent that our budget would not stretch to fill this need. Also, we knew, through our heavy use of picture book bulk loans from the system headquarters collection, that the CBLS collection contained only quality material. I began looking for other libraries who would be willing to form a CCM for children's collection. Another factor influencing my decision was that, despite the fact that CBLS had not updated their collection since 1987, children's popular reading books do not become as "dated" as popular reading adult material. Last and not least was the financial factor—this was a "two for one deal" and as a low budget library the trustees agreed we should "go for it!"

CBLS Resource Sharing Consultant, Georgine Olson, gave me a list of four other libraries in the system who also took bulk loans of a large num-ber of children's books in the course of a year. I contacted these librarians and set up a meeting. With guidance from system personnel, the five libraries formed a CCM plan for Easy materials that was approved by headquarters to deaccess approximately 700 books from their collection. The Chatsworth library took 200 books. Within the original guidelines of the CCM plan, each library tried to designate an area in which they hoped to upgrade their own collection. The problem was that too many wanted to upgrade award winners such as Caldecott. When we were selecting the deaccession books it became apparent that this was not going to work because of the limited number of the coveted titles. Consequently, some of us adjusted our original area of collection. For example, Chatsworth extended its selection to include nonfiction books on dinosaurs and other animals.

In preparing for the actual selecting of CBLS deaccessed books for our collection, I again referred to the Fiction Assessment evaluation lists as well as other lists suggested by the CBLS staff and checked the titles against our collection holdings. In this phase of the CBLS Deaccession, our library was able to add 200 new, quality titles to our collection.

The libraries involved in the Easy Book CCM program mark newly purchased material as sell; just as CBLS deaccessed material with a large "E" spine label. This is very helpful when locating books for the rotating loan. Each library was also responsible for providing a complete list of books that are a part of the CCM program, including author, title, and call number (when applicable) to the other four libraries and CBLS. Fifty books from each collection are rotated among the Easy Coop libraries four times a year. A list of titles included in each "loan" accompanies the shipment. There is a set rotation schedule among the libraries. The CBLS delivery system transports the circulating books. Each library is also responsible for damages or losses that occur to circulating material while it is at their library.

The libraries meet once a year to evaluate and revise the CCM plan. At our most recent meeting, the plan was revised with each library agreeing to purchase a minimum of ten books in a selected picture book/easy reader genre or subject area. As an example, Chatsworth will purchase books, which can be either fiction or non-fiction, about dinosaurs and other non-domestic animals.

Since joining the Easy book CCM plan, I have reorganized our Easy books into the following divisions: Easy picture books, Easy Reader books, and Easy nonfiction. The reason for this reorganization is to make the Easy collection more accessible for the patron (parent, teacher, or child). More accessibility has meant greater circulation and less time spent by the librarian locating material for the patron. The latter is important since we usually have only one person on duty in the library at a time.

CBLS offered two more deaccession opportunities, Phase II and Phase III, for libraries to select books. The Chatsworth library took advantage of these opportunities and added more books in the Easy, Juvenile, and Adult Collections. For instance, because of the fiction assessment and tracking fiction genre circulation, I realized that there were more mystery readers than I had previously thought. Therefore, 100 mysteries were part of the deaccession collection that came to Chatsworth. Other material selections were guided in a similar way by what I had learned about collection assessment and management through participation in the fiction project.

The Forrest District Library, located five miles from Chatsworth, was another participant in the fiction assessment project. Chatsworth and Forrest entered into an informal CCM project involving large print books. Bulk loans of large print books owned by each library are exchanged four times a year. The fact that we both are on the same CBLS delivery route has helped the exchange work well for approximately eighteen months. At that time, both libraries had exhausted the supply of material available. Currently we bulk loan large print materials from the CBLS collection. The need for greater quantities of large print material that created our informal CCM project is still there, and I anticipate that in the near future a more formal large print CCM project will be developed within our geographic area.

SHARED BIBLIOGRAPHIC DATABASES

Membership in these and other CCM projects has increased our library's "collection" without well beyond what our budget would normally allow. However, CCM usually means sharing of bibliographic information. For Chatsworth, that has meant continual typing, updating, and printing of lists to share with its CCM partners. Shared bibliographic access became more and more desirable, but was still beyond the reach of our annual budget.

However, in 1991, our regional automation system—the Resource Sharing Alliance (RSA), added a new level of membership based on a CD-ROM bibliographic database. Once data entry was complete, annual RSA membership and CD-ROM subscription fees would run about $800 to $1,000. While still a stretch for our under $20,000 annual budget, this was an exciting possibility. Participation in the RSA would enable us to have access to millions of titles via the RSA CD-ROM while simultaneously adding our collection to the system. We would be able to fax interlibrary loan requests direct to owning libraries. This would translate into a vastly greater selection of materials and faster service for our patrons.

Then, in 1992, CBLS offered a grant to member libraries in which they would provide the CD-ROM workstation and money towards profiling/training fee. The library would have to find about $5,000 to fund original data entry and commit five years of RSA membership. The Chatsworth Trustees deliberated long about this offer because the annual costs would place a severe strain on our low budget. They finally decided to use money that had been donated to a Library Improvement Fund. We all felt that this opportunity might not present itself again and being a member of this RSA would continue to provide important access to other libraries' collections, especially those in close geographical proximity. Libraries such as ours cannot hope to provide all materials to all patrons. Thus, we are forced to be more creative in the way we budget our finances and we felt this was another form of a CCM plan and an excellent opportunity to increase our service to the community.

We received shipment of our CD-ROM workstation in April 1993. Shortly after it was installed, patrons began to understand how easy it was to locate and personally choose titles not available in our facility. We are currently entering our collection into the database and have begun to receive requests for our materials from other RSA libraries. The CD-ROM database has been invaluable for me, with no formal cataloging training, when I separated the Easy non-fiction from the Easy fiction and began assigning Dewey numbers and subject headings to older titles.

As I reflect on the progress made at this library in the area of cooperative collection management, I can credit our involvement with the fiction assessment grant project and later use of the assessment tool as a positive experience towards better management of our collection. Even though use of the tool will require a time commitment from the staff, I will not hesitate to use it in the future as the need arises—and it seems to arise fairly regularly!

The Conspectus As A Tool For (Cooperative) Collection Management

by Georgine Olson

We, in Illinois, have devoted much time and energy in the last several years to promoting the theories and methods of collection analysis, collection management, and cooperative collection management among our libraries. The conspectus approach to collection management is one we have devoted a great deal of time and effort to teaching and promoting—often using the carrots of grant funding, followed by the sticks of mandated collection analysis.

Sometimes, when another layer of learning or another packet of conspectus forms to fill out descends upon an overworked, underfunded librarian's desk, it just could be that these librarians might well begin to wonder if all this has any practical value to their libraries.

Well, it would be very sad, indeed, if all these tools and methods had little practical value to the average working librarian. Yet, if you are not immersed in the subject—or do not have the time for extensive reading and study in the theories of collection management and cooperative collection management—it is quite possible that it could be difficult to see how the pages and lines and not-quite-right category divisions of a conspectus have any use beyond satisfying some strange delight that higher-ups get from torturing their underlings. And—given the way the Illinois conspectus approach has been developed—those higher-ups are just about anyone who is one step above you in the hierarchy of Illinois library-land.

However, we all recognize that our funding is in no way keeping up with expanding demands for material and information. We have to get much smarter about the way we manage our funds. Since a significant portion of our funds go to collection building—and another sizeable chunk goes to collection management, we can no longer afford to intuit our way though collection management. Economic reality is forcing even the most generously funded of libraries to be a lot more knowledgeable and careful about how funds are dispensed and how collections are maintained.

Libraries are trying any and all methods they can find to help them manage their collections more effectively and efficiently. They perform community surveys to see what it is that library users and non-users want from the library. They run patron use studies to see what it is patrons find useful—or not so useful—in their collections. They sample their holdings for age and frequency of use. They analyze their collections using recommended or self-designed conspectus-type tools. They gamely tackle conspectus sections that ask them to determine not only the quality of their current collection, but their current acquisition levels and future goals.

In my position as a resource sharing consultant for a multitype regional library system, I have been more or less immersed in a variety of conspectus-based, in-house, and cooperative collection management projects since late 1987. Gradually, I began to realize that many of our librarians could not even see the top of their particular tree, much less the forest. So, in the Spring of 1993 I developed yet another chart for our librarians to fill out. However, this one was pure-

Georgine Olson is Resource Sharing Consultant for Corn Belt Library System in Bloomington, Illinois, a multitype regional cooperative serving 64 member libraries.

ly designed to help them see the whole picture—and to show, graphically, that the conspectus was just a part, albeit an important part, of a whole range of activities designed to give them a better handle on their collections—and helping them develop collections that best serve their patrons and their needs.

A sample of these charts are shown on the next pages. The first sample chart is a Non-Fiction Overview; the second is a Fiction Overview followed by a Key explaining the different columns. Because the chart was primarily aimed at small libraries, the subject, genre, class, and media listed are very basic. However, the subject divisions are those used in the first level of the WLN-based Illinois Conspectus and the Fiction Assessment Project.—both of which are familiar to most of our librarians. This type of chart is easily adapted to the most complex of collections, and could be expanded or tailored to use with any conspectus in order to meet the needs of libraries or library consortia of all sizes and kinds.

When completed, the chart gives the library a visual representation of the collection as it is now and as it being used. As librarians fill in different portions of the chart, they will see areas where they might wish to make changes in collection management and development.

The chart is also meant to be used for planning or reviewing cooperative collection management projects. It is hard for cooperating libraries to have a clear picture of each other's collection and its use. As much as narrative statements and library-to-library visits might help, the use of this type of chart can be much more specific to the collections involved. Librarians from any sized library would have a common frame of reference for several facets of collection management and use important to cooperative projects. We did learn, in cooperative collection management projects involving multitype libraries of widely varying sizes, that sometimes percentages worked better than straight numbers. When a library with 1.4 million volumes is participating in a project

---

KEY: COLLECTION OVERVIEW CHARTS

The left-hand column on each page represents the 24 basic subject areas based on the collection analysis conspectus used in Illinois plus a few that have seemed useful to participants in CBLS projects. One page is devoted to non-fiction and the second page to fiction and non-print media.

Below are explanations for the various columns across the top of the chart:

HOLDINGS #/LEVEL	put the # of titles you have in this area and/or, if you have done a formal collection analysis, the conspectus level (i.e. 1, 2a, etc)
AQ LEVEL	Acquisition Level. Again, for those completing formal collection analysis, the level at which new materials are being added.
# NON BOOK	the number of titles you have in the area that are not in book format, i.e. audio cassettes, microform, videos
WHEN WEEDED	write the year this collection was last weeded
COL POLICY	indicate if you have a formal collection policy dealing with this area
CCM AREA	indicate if this area is part of a formal cooperative collection management plan in which you participate
CCM RESPON	indicate if this area is one in which you purchase additional materials as part of a cooperative collection management agreement
HEAVY ILL	indicate if this is an area which you *borrow* heavily on interlibrary loan
HEAVY REF	indicate if your patrons ask many reference questions in this area
USER REQ	indicate if your patrons frequently ask about titles you do not own in this area

Library _____

Date _____

NON-FICTION OVERVIEW

	HOLDINGS #/LEVEL	AQ LEVEL	# NON BOOK	WHEN WEEDED	COL POLICY	CCM AREA	CCM RESPON	HEAVY ILL	HEAVY REF	USER REQ
NON-FICTION										
AG										
ANTHRO										
ART										
BIOLOGY										
BSNS & ECON										
CHEMISTRY										
COMPUTER										
EDUCATION										
ENG & TECH										
GEN STUD										
GEOGRAPHY										
HISTORY										
LANG & LIT										
LAW										
MATH										
MEDICINE										
MUSIC										
PERFORM										
PHIL & REL										
PHYS ED										
PHYS SCI										
POLY SCI										
PSYCH										
SOCIOLOGY										
REFERENCE										
PERIODICALS										
LT NON FIC										
J NON FICTION										
J EASY NON FIC										

Library _____
Date _____

FICTION OVERVIEW

	HOLDINGS #/LEVEL	AQ LEVEL	# NON BOOK	WHEN WEEDED	COL POLICY	CCM AREA	CCM RESPON	HEAVY ILL	HEAVY REF	USER REQ
GENERAL FIC										
ADVENTURE										
CLASSICS										
FANTASY										
HISTORICAL										
HORROR										
MYSTERY										
ROMANCE										
SCI FI										
WESTERNS										
SHORT STORIES										
J FICTION										
J EASY FIC										
LARGE TYPE										
AUDIO										
VIDEO										

with libraries having 200,000 or 20,000 volumes—and all three have the same percentage of business-related holdings *and* reference questions—they have a lot more in common than raw numbers would indicate.

When you read the other articles in this section, you will be introduced to libraries having complete collection management and/or cooperative collection management plans, of which a conspectus-based collection analysis is an integral part. In some other sections and case studies, a complete, comprehensive plan might have been hinted at or envisioned, but these last libraries have put all the pieces together into an official plan to which the institution is committed to use in working with and developing its collec-

tion to best meet the needs of its defined patron community. Whether or not an actual "Olson Overview Chart" was used, its components were and are still part of their processes. The common thread and the framework which holds the plans together is the conspectus.

If you think about it, a conspectus-based approach to collection management, cooperative or stand-alone, is about the most neutral, nonjudgmental way available to study library collections. There is no universal right, wrong, good, bad, pass, or fail grade other than what the library gives itself. It is based on your vision of your library. And, if you should happen to give yourself a failing grade, the conspectus will tell you how to pass the collection management test the next time!

Employing Collection Management As An Institutional Change Agent

by Thomas J. Dorst

I n its most basic aspects, the process of identifying and selecting materials for a library's collection has not seen substantial change in a century. Fundamentally, selection involves the informed judgment of an individual being applied to the available universe of "published" knowledge, in order to build a coherent collection of materials that will serve the needs of a discrete clientele. While this may seem deceptively simple in concept, its perfection in practice has consumed many distinguished careers.

Two persistent institutions have acted to stabilize the selection environment. The first is the library, with its inherently conservative character. For a wide range of reasons that are beyond the scope of this discussion, libraries are evolutionary, rather than revolutionary, agents within their campuses, businesses, or communities. The second institution, the publishers as producers of information, also exists in a well-established niche, even if its stock-in-trade now includes CDs, microforms, electronic journals, and multimedia wonders. Market pressures and the complex relationship between the creators and the publishers of written art and scholarship have historically made the publishing industry wary of rash behavior.

There are signs that the stability of both the library service industry and the traditional publisher as the primary manufacturer of information may be entering a transitional period. The much discussed—if rarely observed—virtual library promises to be both an undefined and unmanaged entity for a considerable period of time to come. Similarly, the economics and means of producing "information" are no longer completely the domain of traditional publishers. Everything from tax laws and corporate takeovers to electronic networks have conspired to atomize information production and make publishing subject to pressures that have little to do with the core function of recording and selling knowledge.

ILLINOIS STATE LIBRARY

Historical Context

Founded in 1839, the Illinois State Library has had a series of missions. It was originally a small collection of legal volumes, maintained for the convenience of legislators and to support the limited executive functions of state government. The State Library remained content with this role into the early 20th century. During the first half of the 20th century, the State Library evolved into a major lending library for the citizens of the state. At one time the State Library had one of the largest collections of children's literature in the state. There were also extensive holdings of fiction and a strong foreign language collection. These materials were loaned to public libraries throughout the state to supplement local collections.

With the creation of a comprehensive network of regional library systems in Illinois in the 1960s in concert with the advent of ILLINET (the statewide, multitype resource sharing network), the State Library gradually redefined itself as a specialized research library. It continued to fulfill its statutory mandate to serve the information needs of state government. As the role of govern-

---

Thomas J. Dorst is Associate Director for Library Services at the Illinois State Library, Springfield, Illinois.

ment has broadened, so has the scope of the State Library's programs and services.

Mission and Collections

The Illinois State Library today is one of the largest state agency libraries in the United States. It has a broad mandate to serve all of state government, as well as participate in a comprehensive statewide resource sharing network: ILLINET. It has holdings in excess of 1.3 million volumes, including the state's regional federal documents depository, a Patent and Trademark depository, the principal Illinois state documents depository, and a map collection of distinction. Subject strengths include public policy, government, politics, standards and regulations, patents and intellectual property, and maps. The Library has over 2,500 current periodical subscriptions and overall holdings of over 5,800 journal titles in paper and microform. In the last two years the Library has begun to acquire extensive CD-ROM holdings, primarily through the federal documents depository program along with with commercial products that augment its reference service.

The State Library is a member of the Illinois Library Computer Systems Organization (ILCSO) and utilizes *ILLINET ONLINE* (IO) as its online catalog and circulation system. The Library is in the process of mounting an extensive local area network, which will eventually tie together IO, CD-ROMs, and other online resources, such as OCLC and the Internet. In addition, the State Library will be installing a geographic information system (GIS) to take maximum service advantage of its cartographic and electronic government information resources.

COLLECTION MANAGEMENT AT ISL PRIOR TO 1990

From the mid-1960s through the mid-1980s, the Illinois State Library enjoyed nearly 20 years of significant collection growth. Materials budgets were stable and adequate. The selection process was guided by a general selection policy, last revised in 1984. In the 1960s and 70s, the Library operated an extensive monographic vendor approval plan. The approval plan was augmented with a variety of standing orders and serial continuations placed directly with publishers. Relatively little direct selection and ordering of monographs was done by staff.

In the second half of the 1980s the Library's materials budget began to tighten, due to the state's general economic recession. At the same time, the volume of publishing and the price of materials continued to rise dramatically while

many new formats of material emerged. Furthermore, the mission of the State Library continued its gradual shift away from fiction, children's' material, and general interest nonfiction as important elements in its collecting strategy.

Given these circumstances, it is not at all surprising that the State Library's collection management program became unbalanced. The approval plan shifted from book approvals to slips and finally was canceled altogether. In the years immediately preceding the implementation of the current collection management process in 1990, monographs were obtained predominantly as continuations or through standing orders. A small number of the staff determined how any uncommitted funds would be spent. Due to the exigencies of state agency funding, these decisions often had to be made very late in the budget year, leading to purchases intended to meet fiscal circumstances moreso than collection-related service needs.

The nature of journal selection and maintenance also underwent significant change as fiscal circumstances changed in the late 1980s. It should be noted that a significant portion of the periodical collection is comprised of depository titles from the state and federal governments. These resources were not subject to the fiscal dislocations described below. However, they are very much part of the space and access considerations that impelled the design and implementation of a new collection management program.

During the 20 years prior to 1986, the trade periodical collection enjoyed considerable stability. There were sufficient funds to maintain title runs and add titles as deemed necessary. The primary problem was space in the State Library's overcrowded facility. Consequently, a significant portion of the materials budget was utilized to acquire microform backfiles of serials, rather than binding paper copies. In 1986, there was a significant budget cut resulting in major periodical cancellations. The decision was made to cancel many current titles for which film was available and to obtain titles only in film. This unbalanced the overall service program because the mission of the Library was shifting heavily to the provision of very current and topical information in support of government operations. A periodical collection with the most current issues of many important titles being 18 to 24 months old was problematic.

The final element of note in the organization and operation of collection management at the Illinois State Library prior to 1990 was the use of staff in the process. With the heavy dependence on a trade book approval plan, a stable periodicals list, and the predominance of depository documents, the Library can be fairly characterized as operating under an acquisitions-process model prior to 1990. Professional staff members had no subject-specific selection assignments as part of their job responsibilities. Reference staff were responsible for requesting items for the reference collection. Any staff member could request a title for the general collection, but there was no mechanism for ensuring total subject coverage nor was there a mechanism to report back on requests beyond monitoring the new arrival shelves.

Focusing collection building on the technical aspects of acquisitions was exacerbated by the need to expend state funds in a proscribed manner and time frame. This is not in any way to suggest that the acquisitions-process model was inadequate when it was instituted or that staff members were abdicating their responsibilities. Rather, it is a model that many libraries exhibited when funds were relatively plentiful. The Illinois State Library is a classic example of how an acquisitions-process model breaks down when funding is significantly reduced, the automatic functions of approval plans and standing orders are eliminated, and the service mission is changed without clear purpose and explicit articulation.

COLLECTION MANAGEMENT AT ISL AFTER 1990

As the Illinois State Library entered the 1990s, it underwent a number of substantial changes that led to a comprehensive revision of its collection management program. The first, and most visible, change was when the Library moved into a new 167,000 square foot building. This was the first building devoted solely to library functions in the 150-year history of the Illinois State Library. The five floors of compact shelving virtually eliminated collection space problems and allowed the reconsideration of many collection maintenance and preservation practices. As part of the move to the new facility, the State Library also replaced its stand-alone circulation system and catalog with ILLINET Online, the statewide, multi-institution automation system.

At the same time the State Library moved into its new building, Illinois' economy reached the bottom of its recession. Further complicating the picture, the State Library underwent two substantial staff downsizings in two years. In the first instance, an early retirement program was instituted throughout state government. While popular and easy to implement in strained economic times, early retirement programs provide little or no coherent way to manage which functional

areas are affected by the staff departures at the unit level. Consequently, the state government early retirement program resulted in the loss of several library staff members with long experience. In the second instance, the size of the Library's authorized staff complement was reduced. While no layoffs were necessary, the ability to fill even the most critical vacancies was severely diminished.

In order to deal with the staff reductions, the library operational units underwent two reorganizations between 1990 and 1993. In the first, the technical services—including acquisitions, government documents, cataloging, serials, and collection management—were combined into a single division under an associate director, who reported, in turn, the Deputy Director. The other areas of the library—including reference, interlibrary loan, circulation, and automated services—remained separate units, each reporting to the Library's Deputy Director. Subsequently, the entire library services component of the State Library was organized into a single division with four principal units: Public Services, Collection Access, Documents, and Collection Management. Each of these units is managed by a coordinator reporting to one associate director. This new Library Services Division joined the established Library Development Group and Literacy Office as the primary functional elements of the Illinois State Library.

As the recession eased, the materials budget of the Library also stabilized and made modest gains after 1990. The available funding became marginally adequate, given the service mission of the Library. There emerged an obvious need to rearrange funding priorities, rather than make additional, large-scale cuts.

All of these factors led to the decision in 1990 to replace the acquisitions-process model of operation with a collection management model. Initially, time was devoted to understanding the existing pattern of expenditure and collection building. There was also the commitment to replace the 1984 selection policy with a comprehensive, subject-based collection management policy. Finally, it was decided that professional staff would be assigned subject selection responsibilities for the general collection. The acquisition and management of the federal and state documents elements of the collection remained under the control of the Documents Coordinator. However, those resources, and their subsequent role in the service program, was to be explicitly reflected in the collection management policy for the first time.

The new collection management model was implemented incrementally over four years:

1990-1993. During the bulk of the first year, service and collection definitions were revised and clarified. For the first time, the Illinois State Library explicitly stated that it was a special library, serving a government clientele. It was made clear to staff that the collecting focus would be adjusted to meet the expectations of that mission. The State Library's role as an ILLINET participant was not abandoned but it was clearly stated that collections would not be built solely to serve resource sharing needs.

While there was concern that this would appear to be a retreat from the Library's traditional role as a designated, state Reference and Research Center, experience has shown otherwise. Since 1990, the State Library has seen annual growth in requests filled for other libraries in Illinois and is now one of the largest percentage net lenders in ILCSO. There is now general agreement that it is essential for a special library to have a well defined and articulated service mission in order to participate effectively in the resource sharing environment.

While the process of establishing a definition for its service mission—and concomitantly its collection management—was in progress, the Library's expenditure patterns and assumptions were analyzed for the preceding five years. As described above, it was discovered that too many decisions were made to try and maintain collections that served an overly generalized service mission that could no longer be sustained. Furthermore, the established acquisitions-process model placed a premium on the timing of purchases, rather than their relevance to current collection needs.

Substantial resources were devoted to standing orders and continuations. In many instances, these materials were directed to the reference collection. As a result, the reference collection had become unmanageable while the general collection had suffered serious neglect. These circumstances, along with the periodical collecting emphasis on maintaining title runs, were at fundamental odds with the definition of a special library—i.e., collecting to serve the current and topical information needs of state government.

Beginning in 1990, steps were taken to bring collection building into balance with the newly stated service mission. The first step was to better define the reference collection and impose limits on the proportion of the materials budget devoted to that element of the collection. This effort is still in progress but there is now a separate accounting for reference materials and the amount devoted to reference materials is controlled. Furthermore, the existing reference collection has undergone comprehensive review

and more government documents have been brought in to augment the service program.

CONSPECTUS-BASED COLLECTION ASSESSMENT

Also in 1990, the drafting of a comprehensive collection management policy was begun. It was decided to include both general and subject specific selection criteria. The policy was designed to control the weeding and preservation functions, as well as collection building. Finally, it was decided that the content of the policy should be based on a thorough collection assessment, employing the Research Libraries Group (RLG) Conspectus methodology. This was a fundamental departure for the Illinois State Library and marked the clear demarcation between the old acquisitions-process model and the new collection management model. As such, it presented a formidable challenge to convince the staff of the value of qualitative collection analysis.

With the State Library's move to ILLINET Online, participation in the Illinois Collections Analysis Matrix (ICAM) project became a viable option for conducting a systematic collection assessment. The ICAM project is a local variation of the conspectus approach to collection analysis. The 495 subject categories in the ICAM were chosen as a consortially manageable alternative to the several thousand subjects in the RLG Conspectus. ILCSO-member libraries were invited to analyze their collections and submit data to a union database. The intent was to build cooperative collecting initiatives utilizing this common frame of reference. Regardless of the number and arrangement of subjects, the ICAM, like the RLG Conspectus, required the qualitative assessment of collections by knowledgeable staff and an understanding of the RLG defined indicators for collection strength and collecting intensity.

After some preliminary investigations to ensure that the State Library's collection could be effectively assessed, it was divided into approximately two-dozen broad subject categories. These were a combination of ICAM categories, such as Art and Architecture, and categories with specific relevance to the State Library, such as Government. The 495 ICAM subjects were assigned to appropriate categories and staff were assigned one or more categorical assessment responsibilities. Initially, collection analysis responsibilities were given to professional staff in the Reference Unit; Library Services Division unit managers; and selected other professional staff who had expressed a specific interest in participating in the process.

It was made clear that the result of the assessment would be a comprehensive written policy and that the selection of materials would become a delegated staff function. Even with the prospect of having direct control over the selection of materials, staff members were extremely reluctant to perform qualitative assessments. Beyond the lack of confidence in subjective collection analysis, which is a typical response to the introduction of conspectus analysis, the State Library staff were unsure how their analysis would be used in the redefinition of the service mission. Specifically, they were concerned that the collection analysis, when combined with a clearly articulated special library mission, would lead to large-scale collection weeding in the humanities, arts, hard sciences, and selected social science disciplines.

While the division managers were not able to totally alleviate staff concerns, there was a concerted effort to assure the newly appointed selectors that they would also have a say in the withdrawal process and that no large-scale withdrawals would be undertaken until the collection policy was in place. In addition, several training sessions in qualitative analysis were held. To augment the qualitative analysis, available statistics on collection size, circulation, and inter-loan activity were gathered and arranged in the assessment subjects. Over approximately nine months in 1990 and 1991, the State Library staff prepared their analyses and submitted conspectus worksheets to the coordinator of collection management and the division's associate director.

As the analysis process progressed, the first attempt to institute subject selection was initiated. Nominal funds were made available to each selector in 1991. Selectors were instructed to select only monographs and to be conservative in determining what would be in scope for the general collection. All of these initial selections were reviewed by managers. It soon became apparent that the collection analysis being done by staff provided them with a good perspective on the nature of the existing collection. Few selections were rejected as being obviously out-of-scope, even in the first round of fund allocations.

To supplement the incipient selection process and reinforce the new definition of the collection, a new approval plan was instituted in 1991. Primarily employing slips and setting conservative parameters on coverage, the plan was presented to selectors when the second allocation of funds was made in mid-1991. Additionally, a substantial number of standing orders were eliminated and made subject to selector review and directed order. This freed funds for general collection building and forced selectors to evaluate many titles that had been added to the collection automatically.

The final activity that was undertaken in 1991 was a journal cancellation and fund reallocation for new subscriptions. Unlike the monographic selection process, which was established as a subject specific activity from the inception of the new collection management model, the journal collection was treated as the joint responsibility of all selectors and unit managers. A list of titles that "appeared" to be out-of-scope for a library specializing in current information relevant to a government clientele was prepared. This list was then submitted to selectors for review. They were instructed to provide justification for retaining any title on the list or suggestions of additional titles to cancel. The amended list was then canceled, and the funds generated were reallocated to initiate new subscriptions that were more germane to the Library's mission. Two rounds of cancellations and three rounds of new subscriptions were completed between 1991 and 1993. Almost 15 percent of the original periodical list was canceled and approximately 300 new titles were added. All "film only" subscriptions were also canceled. Current subscriptions were entered for those titles deemed necessary. By mid-1993, the review and selection of periodicals was made a direct subject selector responsibility. Beginning in 1994, the bulk of the collection funds devoted to periodicals will be under the direct control of individual selectors.

With the selection process established and the first complete collection assessment finished, programmatic emphasis was placed on completing the collection management policy. After all appropriate reviews and revisions, the policy was promulgated in June 1993. The policy includes 35 subject categories and somewhat more than the original 495 ICAM subjects. For each general category there is:

1. a subject definition,
2. selection guidelines on scope, depth, format restrictions, and existing areas of collection strength,
3. a detailed conspectus analysis for each specific subject within the category,
4. general comments,
5. an estimation of the State Library's audience for the subject, and
6. suggested referrals for more information.

With the distribution of the collection management policy to selectors and other staff at the State Library, the framework for the collection management model was completed. Save some residual staff resistance to the overall evolution of the State Library's mission, the last vestiges of the acquisitions-process model have been eliminated or are quickly atrophying. In the next fiscal year's materials budget allocation, virtually all expenditure will be under the control of subject selectors. They will be guided by the written policy and their own judgment to build a sound and useful resource. In addition, the initial collection assessments will be revised and augmented. Staffmembers are now in a much better position to perform the assessments in a consistent manner. In areas of collection emphasis, such as government, politics, and the social sciences, the qualitative analysis may be expanded to the full subject levels of the RLG Conspectus.

THE FUTURE

There remain several activities to be initiated in the State Library's collection management program. Although the service mission of the Library has evolved, the existing collection has undergone only the most casual reshaping. For example, when a quantity of microform periodicals were discovered to be in need of cataloging, appropriate subject selectors were asked to review them and make recommendations on their retention. As a result, several hundred titles were withdrawn from the collection because they were now out-of-scope, thus saving the cost of cataloging. The review and weeding process needs to be extended to the entire general collection and made a systematic part of the selectors' responsibilities.

Likewise, the preservation of the State Library's collection is in a rudimentary state. The collection management program must be extended to accommodate the regular preservation review of the collection. Furthermore, the collection management policy should be augmented to identify preservation needs in the collection. Because funds are not available, the incorporation of preservation analysis into the collection management program has proceeded slowly.

What has just been described is the transition from one method of operation to another, more viable method for the present. The lingering question is what comes next. For the Illinois State Library, as a large special library, the answer is not completely obvious.

The State Library has a significant collection resource with which to provide service. State and federal documents provide a solid and stable core. However, the general collection—like that of virtually every other library—cannot fully meet the needs of the State Library's users. This is a commentary, not only on the funds available to build collections over the last few years, but also on the nature and scope of the modern information environment. There is just too much information, in too many forms, for one institution to acquire and manage, no matter how circumscribed its mission.

The Illinois State Library has begun to examine the basic assumptions that have separated collection building from the overlapping realms of interlibrary loan, document delivery, and resource sharing. Such assumptions have led to distinct budgetary categorizations for materials and online services. They have also led to organizational distinctions between collection management, interlibrary loan, and online searching. We are no longer confident that these distinctions have relevance.

In the same way that users can now locate and manipulate data in a computer file as needed, libraries will have to accommodate the selection and acquisition of resources on a transactional basis. In other words, the future will see libraries "purchasing" an article or a data file when a patron requests it, rather than through the predictive methods of the collection management model just implemented. An entirely different set of selector skills will have to be employed to build collections in such an environment. In fact, large, generalized collections may not be routinely built at all in the future. Some of the Illinois State Library's collection likely will not exist as a physical item in the library until a patron expresses a need for specific information and the "collection" may well walk out the door with the patron, never to grace the library's shelves or see the inside of a bindery.

Few activities or practices disappear totally in libraries. They are—and will continue to be—conservative social institutions. The collection management model now operating at the Illinois State Library has subsumed, rather than eliminated, aspects of the previous acquisitions-process model. In turn, the collection management model will give way to a collecting methodology more electronic in character and more virtual in philosophy. The challenge is to prepare staff and design services to take maximum advantage of that environment.

Cooperative Collection Management Among Four Rural Libraries

by Ruth Shasteen

Four libraries in East-Central Illinois established a model cooperative collection development project funded by a Library Services and Construction Act (LSCA) Grant for the purpose of determining if the theory of cooperative collection development could actually be put into practice, specifically in the case of small rural libraries. The project proved to be very successful, demonstrating that theory can work in real situations. Cooperative collection development is a practical solution to problems created by underfunding, inadequate or underdeveloped collections, and long delivery times for interlibrary loans. This article will describe the demonstration project, the methods used to assess the collections, and the process of writing the cooperative plan.

THE PROJECT

Atwood-Hammond Public Library District (Atwood, Illinois), Marrowbone Public Library District (Bethany, Illinois), Lovington Public Library District (Lovington, Illinois), and Elizabeth Titus Memorial Library (Sullivan, Illinois) were the four libraries involved in this cooperative project aimed at exploring the practicalities of cooperative collection management in small rural libraries. The ultimate purpose of the project was to provide better service to the collective clientele of the cluster's service area in a timely and cost effective manner through a coordinated collection development plan. The four members of the cluster also sought to demonstrate the validity and feasibility of cooperative efforts for other small rural libraries. Further, we hoped to improve materials access and speed of delivery. We would use telefacsimile to transmit requests for materials. We would take full advantage of our membership in a shared online system coordinated by the regional library system, Rolling Prairie Library System, headquarterd in Decatur, Illinois. We also hoped to speed delivery by making better use of the system's library materials delivery service.

To accomplish the goals, the librarians first consulted with Barbara Allen, the cooperative collection management consultant at the Illinois State Library. Ms. Allen introduced the group to the process of collection assessment developed by the Pacific Northwest Conspectus, now used in the WLN Conspectus and the basis of the Illinois conspectus database.

The cluster libraries decided to follow those collection analysis methods recommended by the Illinois State Library, using the WLN Conspectus worksheets. The worksheets are available for both Dewey and Library of Congress classification, and in basic and detailed forms. The basic Dewey forms were found to be the best suited for the collection analysis of our four small libraries. Analysis methods included gathering title counts and circulation information for each subject area. There are 24 subject areas covered by the basic worksheets.

The WLN data sheets did not, however, provide as much room to record information as we wanted for this project. The consensus among the librarians involved was that there is much more in determining the total picture of a collection than title and circulation counts. Although space for comments is provided on the WLN work

Ruth Shasteen is Director of Elizabeth Titus Memorial Library in Sullivan, Illinois.

sheets, we chose to design a form which allowed even more information to be recorded in one area. The new form that was created includes more space for video, audio, periodicals, realia, and other information. The form could also be used to record notes on community interest and support, data on reference requests in that area, circulation figures, the number of interlibrary loan requests, and other pertinent statistics. The total assessment of all types of materials was necessary to accurately assess subject area strengths.

Another set of worksheets was developed based on the WLN format but differed by using the Dewey divisions only (i.e., 000-099, 100-199, etc.). WLN uses specific classification numbers from several divisions to cover a particular subject area. For this group of libraries, this method was not very effective because the four library collections are relatively small and therefore did not cover all the classifications in the WLN forms and, conversely, some that were present in the cluster libraries' collections were not listed on the forms. The new worksheets allowed more flexibility to analyze each collection.

Through the analysis process, each librarian reached a better understanding of not only the strengths and weaknesses in her own library collection, but also by working closely with each other, he or she gained an increased knowledge of the neighboring libraries' collections. This was an important part of the cooperation among the cluster libraries.

After analysis, the four librarians met to determine the primary collection responsibilities. A cooperative spirit was really needed for this part. Each library decided its top priorities for collection development, its current strengths and weaknesses, and considered those in relation to the other cooperating libraries' needs, strengths, and weaknesses. The primary collection responsibilities were divided among the cluster libraries.

Primary collection responsibilities may represent either current subject weaknesses or current strengths. In either case, each library agreed to develop one or more subject areas in depth. Each library agreed to commit to providing materials in that subject area to the other libraries. The key concept was to bring the subject area to the desired level in that one library, taking into consideration not only the home library's needs and clientele but also those of the partner libraries— the subject area was developed to serve the needs of the collective clientele. Being well informed about the collections of all the libraries involved was vital to this process.

Some of the methods this cluster utilized included the exchange of the individual written collection development policies for each library,

the continuous flow of information concerning specific reference requests received in the targeted subject areas, and the exchange of bibliographic data and reviews of materials as possible acquisitions. Again, a cooperative spirit is necessary in the process.

THE POLICIES AND THE COOPERATIVE PLAN

After the collection analysis and determination of primary collection responsibilities were completed, the individual collection development policies were written. Previous policies did exist, but the new ones were standard in form and covered the same information for each library. Each policy contained the library's mission and roles, a description of the community, and the purpose of the collection. A detailed summary of each subject area contained the title of the area (i.e., BIRDS, RELIGION, etc.) followed by the Dewey classification numbers, the current and target collection levels (using the WLN indicators), and a paragraph summarizing the plan for development including such factors as format, language, retrospective collecting, targeted age/reading levels, weeding, chronological periods, and/or geographic areas.

Once the individual plans were in place, the cooperative policy was written. The format was basically the same as the individual library policies with a few added adjustments. The policy begins with a brief mission statement for the cluster, and the purpose of the plan (i.e., who is involved, what they are involved in, and why). Descriptions of participating libraries include location, size, current strengths and weaknesses, a brief description of their clientele, collections, automation levels, and affiliations. A section dealing with the targeted collection areas follows. That section begins with a brief description of how the areas were determined and lists each area with the following information: title, Dewey or LC classification number(s), name of the collecting library, the current collection level, and the target collection level (again using WLN indicators). For each area, a short paragraph identifies the plan for development including the same factors considered in the individual library plans.

The remaining section delineates the responsibilities of each participating library covering the financial and time commitments, reevaluation procedures, statistical records to be kept, materials delivery plan, materials selection with input from other cluster libraries, and bibliographic access.

The adoption page lists the dates of adoption by each of the participating library boards of trustees, and has the signatures of the librarians and an official from each library board. Appendixes include the collection development policies of each of the participating libraries and other pertinent documents such as the Library Bill of Rights and the Freedom to Read and View statements.

COOPERATION AND SHARING

Although these four libraries have a strong history of informal cooperation and sharing, the formalization and documentation of the cooperative effort is a sound practice, for boards of trustees change and librarians move on. In our case, the purpose of the formalization process was: to ensure the continuation of the cooperative venture, to clarify the responsibilities of those involved, and to justify the selection policy to any interested party.

A great deal of thought and effort went into the development of this model cooperative project, and into the improvement of each library's collection analysis and development. Documenting the scope and direction of a collection is an excellent way to focus on what is ultimately needed for a particular library's situation. All four librarians involved with this project reported that they knew more about their own libraries and partner libraries, and could make better selection decisions because of that knowledge.

When trying to locate materials and information for patrons, each librarian has found the task easier by being able to identify a nearby location for specific subject strengths. Utilizing the available methods of document delivery (state and regional delivery services, telefacsimile, and local exchange) has made the time much shorter between the initial requests and filling them. Patrons are better informed about the choices of materials available to them through the use of selected bibliographies in the target subject areas.

SUMMARY

It is important to keep in mind that this cooperative project involved analysis of the total collection in each library, writing individual as well as a cooperative plan, actual selection and acquisition of materials in the targeted subject areas, and the development of bibliographies. Not every cooperative project needs to be this involved.

This project was established with a specific purpose in mind—to examine the theory of cooperative collection development in small rural libraries. This project was successful and did prove that theory can be put into practice. The librarians involved did make adjustments in the process to suit the specific situation, although the information entered into the Illinois conspectus database was uniform and consistent in format and content with what others around the state enter. Librarians looking toward cooperative planning should focus on their own libraries' needs and situation as a first step in the process.

In addition to suiting the project to local needs, the financial commitment should be examined. More money is not always necessary in cooperative efforts. The libraries involved were able to make a formal financial commitment for a specific time period because the funds were already available. With a cooperative plan, the library is able to redirect funds. Instead of having to spread the materials budget to all subject areas, libraries will focus on targeted areas and acquire basic minimal levels in others.

Territorialism seems to be strong in many libraries around the country. Being overly possessive of materials can be a real obstacle to providing quality library service. This cluster of librarians found that the support available from the group can mean a big difference in the kind of service available to the patrons. Being able to rely on help from a partner library to cover the gaps in your collection without having to purchase the same materials as the other libraries, and knowing that these materials will be available quickly improves service dramatically. Entering into cooperative agreements with the idea of giving as well as receiving will enable these joint projects to have a reasonable chance for success and provide many benefits to all involved.

Any type of library can be involved in such projects. A natural alliance would seem to be one between a school and a public library in the same community. The logistics of making such a plan work would be much easier with less distance to deal with, *and* the clientele would be similar. As an example, school/public library cooperation in the same town could involve developing a single subject area in-depth at different age levels in each partner library. By finding a mutually agreeable subject area and building from there based on local needs, the community would have a strong, comprehensive coverage of that topic.

Cooperative collection development can happen in libraries of all types and sizes if those involved are intent on sharing and cooperating to provide a solution to limited funds and lack of materials and resources. This approach can ultimately provide better, more cost effective service to the community.

Process To Promise: The CCM Plan

by Brenda J. Foote

Some libraries have the resources to provide all the services necessary for entertainment, cultural, and educational development in their communities, while others are struggling to keep their doors open. Some have had their budgets frozen or cut. Others have been able to maintain a minimal amount of growth in their budgets. Regardless of circumstance, most libraries have been unable to adjust their budgets to keep up with the inflation of book and journal prices. Now, and in the future, we need to develop cooperative collection plans to address continued pressures on already strained acquisitions budgets.

Since informational needs of rural residents do not differ significantly from those in urban areas, our goal, as a group of small libraries in rural Illinois, is to ensure that children growing up in our communities are afforded the same access to information and resources as children in urban communities. In our case, the only way to be sure this goal became a reality was to develop a plan for combining and sharing resources: *the cooperative collection management plan.*

FIRST STEPS

The first step in developing our cooperative collection management plan was to define our purpose and set goals and objectives to meet that purpose. Secondly, we identified prospective project participants. Nine Illinois libraries representing our small, rural area of Southwestern Illinois agreed to participate: Central Public Library, Chester Public Library, Coulterville Public Library, Cutler Public Library, Evansville Public Library, Marissa Public Library, Pinckneyville Public Library, Sparta Public Library, and the Steeleville District Library. Together these libraries serve citizens living in a 625 square mile area.

It was the intent of the cluster to improve our ability to provide on-site access to materials most in demand in the most cost-effective and timely manner possible as well as becoming more proficient in the use of reference resources.

Our objectives were to evaluate our reference collections using the WLN Conspectus, build our collections using "target" areas and demand-oriented selection, and, finally, improve reference service and collections by developing and implementing a comprehensive cooperative collection management plan.

CONSPECTUS AS PROCESS

As Director of the Sparta Public Library, I felt it was imperative to assess our collection to identify our library's strengths and weaknesses. We used the WLN conspectus database worksheets, which are evaluation tools for assessing qualitative information regarding strengths of specific subject collections. Through a Library Services and Construction Act funded contract with WLN, worksheets were provided by the Illinois State Library to the Illinois regional library system agencies and were then made available to member libraries upon request. Based on our library's collection, I chose the second level conspectus worksheets. Level Two has 500 categories of subjects within the 24 main divisions. I included staff and board members in the evaluation process

Brenda J. Foote is Director of the Sparta Public Library in Sparta, Illinois.

because we believed this would give everyone an opportunity to develop and apply newly-learned skills in collection development. It allowed each of us to become familiar with all of the library's resources. Finally, we believed assessment would help us develop further expertise in the use of reference collections.

I held two inservice meetings. Each staff and board member was given:

1. a sample copy of a complete conspectus worksheet—Dewey,
2. an information sheet describing collection level indicators (adapted from the *RLG Collection Development Manual,* 2nd ed., and the State of Alaska Intensity Codes), and
3. an information sheet on "Reference Types" as well as a sheet on "Weeding at the Library" (from the *Handbook for Small, Rural, and Emerging Public Libraries* by Anne Gervasi).

When we began our project, I explained the conspectus worksheets and the process of assessment. Each employee and board member was given the option of choosing both a subject area with which they were familiar and an area they knew very little about. For example, one of the board members is a social studies teacher, so he chose an appropriate subject area—Division: HISTORY AND AUXILIARY SCIENCES: 900–998. However, since he knew little about computers and wanted to become more familiar with the library's resources, he also chose another helpful area—Division: COMPUTER SCIENCE: 003–006; 621.39.

We have a collection of approximately 30,000 volumes. On average, seven to ten staff personnel and board members worked two hours each Saturday before regular library hours for about four weeks. Ten to 15 more hours were volunteered by board members during regular library hours. The staff worked a total of approximately ten paid hours to finish the assessment project.

After the assessments were completed, I compiled, reviewed, and evaluated the conspectus worksheets. During the evaluation I also identified my "target" areas for purposes of our CCM plan. I took into consideration the interest and demand in some subject areas, the various organizations and occupations in our area, and the expression of need by patrons. The "target" areas I chose are outlined in table 1.

COLLABORATIVE ACTION

Each CCM group member tabulated and presented targeted areas at our next group meeting. We were then able to put together a plan based on targeted areas of each library's collection. The libraries involved in this group agreed to make an ongoing commitment to continued cooperative collection development. We all realized the advantages of this kind of resource sharing, and each library is committed to the continued maintenance of the target areas.

Finally, we developed a plan of responsibility that all participants agreed to follow to ensure that the CCM plan would work. We agreed to continue to meet quarterly to evaluate the CCM plan to ensure its continued success.

TABLE 1

1.	BLACK HISTORY: 302, 305, 326		
	Current assessment level:	1a	minimal level, with uneven coverage
	Acquisition commitment:	2a	basic information level, introductory
	Goal:	2a	basic information level, introductory
2.	LOCAL GENEALOGY: 977, 929		
	Current assessment level:	1b	minimal level, but chosen well
	Acquisitions commitment:	1b	minimal level, but chosen well
	Goal :	2a	basic information level, introductory
3.	BIOGRAPHY: 920		
	Current assessment level:	1a	minimal level, with uneven coverage
	Acquisitions commitment:	2a	basic information level, introductory
	Goal:	2a	basic information level, introductory

(Codes adapted from *RLG Collection Development Manual,* 2nd ed., and the State of Alaska Intensity Codes.)

The participants agreed to the following responsibilities:

1. All materials acquired in the targeted area will be available to the other participating libraries regardless of format. Borrowing libraries may be asked not to circulate some materials, only make them available at their facility. Each lending library reserves the right to refuse to circulate some materials but will make them available at their library for patrons to use.
2. Requested materials will be made available as quickly as possible.
3. Materials may be picked up by patrons using normal reciprocal borrowing procedures after a phone call or E-mail message from the borrowing library has been placed to the lending library. Otherwise, materials will be sent with the next intra-system delivery.
4. Fax transmissions and photocopying will be kept to a minimum due to the costs involved.
5. Each library will be responsible for keeping statistics on loans and any charges incurred for later study by the cluster to determine if revisions need to be made in policies.
6. Each library will be responsive to the needs of the other participating libraries when choosing materials in the targeted areas.
7. Each library is responsible for keeping the other participants informed in a timely manner regarding new acquisitions in the targeted areas.

FROM PROMISE TO PROCESS

Our Cooperative Collection Management Plan has been a resounding success. The exchange of resources among member libraries has exceeded my every expectation. At Sparta, I have been able to develop weaker sections of our collection and "target" areas through budgeting dollars in those areas that would have been spread throughout the entire collection. Because the first year of the public libraries' CCM program was so successful, in the fall of 1993 I worked with the Sparta Lincoln Middle School's library media specialist to develop a similar CCM plan for the entire Sparta School District No. 140 and the Sparta Public Library.

Index

"Access versus ownership" of library materials, 7–8
Acquisitions, 20
Alaska Collection Development Project, 57–60
Alaska Conspectus Consortium, 58
*Alaska Cooperative Collection Development
    Agreement,* 58
Alaska Coordinated Collection Development
    Agreement, 57
Alaska State Library's Interlibrary Cooperative
    Program, 57
Allen, Barbara, 97
AMIGOS, 45
Anchorage Municipal Libraries, collection assessment
    for, 37–38
Assessment Data Worksheet Summary, 73, 76–77, 79
Association of Research Libraries, 11
Atwood-Hammond Public Library District, 97–99
Automated systems, advantages of, 22
Availability of collections, 22

Baker, Sharon, 69–70
Berry, John, 66
Biagini, Mary K., 84
Bibliographic databases, sharing of, 86
Blue Ribbon Committee, 15–16
Books for College Libraries, 3d ed. (BCL3), 59
Books for College Libraries, 3rd Edition (BCL3), 33, 45
Boze, Patricia, 69–70
Bradley University, 19, 21
Bushing, Mary, 46

CCM. *See* Conspectus-based (cooperative) collection
    management
CD-ROM bibliographic database, 86
Chatsworth Township Library
    fiction assessment and, 83–86
Circulation and in-house use statistics, 20
"Collection Analysis Reports," 45
Collection assessment. *See also* Fiction assessment;
    *Krueger Manuals; Krueger Method; WLN
    Conspectus*

fees for service vs., 8
methods of, 8–9
*Collection Assessment Manual for Small- and
    Medium-Sized Libraries,* 73, 78, 79, 81
Collection Development Policy, 46, 47, 56
Collection Development Steering Committee, 57–59
"Collection Management Plan," 47
Collection Planning Worksheet, 65
Collection Profile, Acquisitions, Budget Manual
    (Graham), 69
Colorado, Krueger Method in, 26
Connecticut, Krueger Method in, 26
Conspectus-based (cooperative) collection
    management (CCM). *See also specific topics*
    among rural libraries, 97–99
    theoretical value of, 7–10
Conspectus Database Worksheet (Dewey), 36, 54
Conspectus Database Worksheet (LC), 35
Cooperative Collection Management Plan (CCM
    Plan), 101–3
Cooperative groups, 22
*Coordinated/Cooperative Collection Assessment-
    Version 2.0,* 26–27
Coordinated Cooperative Collection Development for
    Illinois Libraries. *See* Krueger Manuals
Customer service approach, 69–82
    comparison of methods available and, 69–70
    data categories and, 78–80
    data collection and, 78
    formatting the conspectus and, 71–78
    goal of, 70–71
    results, 80

Data collection and analysis of distribution of
    holdings compared with circulation and/or ILL
    requests method, 17
Data Gathering Handbook for Collection Analysis
    (Schmidt), 18, 21
Deaccession CCM Grant Project, 85–86
Dewey decimal classification scheme, 18, 20, 36, 44,
    97–98

Directory of the Illinois Valley Library System, 16

East Peoria Community High School, 19, 21
Elizabeth Titus Memorial Library, 97–99
Expert review of strengths method, 16

Fees for service vs. better management through
    assessment, 8
Fiction assessment, 63–86
    Chatsworth Township Library and, 83–86
    Krueger Method and, 25–27
    quality and demand as basis for, 65–68
Fiction Assessment Data Worksheet, 73–75, 78–80
Fiction Collection Assessment Manual (Baker and
    Boze), 69–70
Fiction Collection Intensity Indicators, 70
Fiction Overview Chart, 88, 90
Fiction Worksheet for Small Public Libraries, 70
Forrest District Library, 86
Fred Meyer Charitable Trust, 58

*Genreflecting: A Guide to Reading Interests in Genre
    Fiction* (Rosenberg), 84
Geographic information system (GIS), 92
Graham, Ruth, 69
"Guidelines for Implementing High Quality Informa-
    tion Services" (Blue Ribbon Committee), 15

Hall, Blaine, 43
Handbook of Contemporary Fiction, A (Biagini), 84
Howser, Ray, 15

ILLINET, 91, 94
ILLINET Cooperative Collection Development
    policies, 15, 17
ILLINET ONLINE (IO), 92–94
Illinois Board of Higher Education, 22
Illinois Collections Analysis Matrix (ICAM) project, 94
Illinois Conspectus, 22–24
Illinois' Corn Belt Library System (CBLS), 25, 33, 69,
    83, 85–86
Illinois Interlibrary Cooperative Project, 16
Illinois Library Computer Systems Organization
    (ILCSO), 92, 94
Illinois Library System (IVLS), 15–21
Illinois State Library (ISL), 17, 18, 92, 97, 101
    collection management (after 1990), 93–94
    collection management (prior to 1990), 92–93
    conspectus-based collection assessment at,
        94–96
    future of, 96
    in historical context, 91–92
    institutional change and, 91–96

mission and collections of, 92
"Implementation of Coordinated/Cooperative
    Collection Development-A Planning Model for
    Systems," 17
Institutional change, collection management and,
    91–96
Interlibrary loan, 20–21

King Research Project, 16–18
Krueger, Karen, 17, 19–20, 26
*Krueger Manuals (Coordinated Cooperative Collec-
    tion Development for* Illinois Libraries), case study
    of, 19–23
Krueger Method, 13–27
    Bloomington-Normal cooperative reference
        services and, 25
    criticism of, 21–22
    fiction assessment and, 25–27
    Illinois Valley Library System and the
        development of, 15–18
    introduction to, 13

Library and Information Resources for the Northwest
    (LIRN) Program, 31, 58
Library holdings checked against standard lists
    method, 16
Library of Congress (LC) subject classification, 11, 18,
    33, 35, 97–98
Library Services and Construction Act (LSCA), 25, 83
Library Services and Construction Act (LSCA) Grant,
    97, 101
Library Services and Construction Act (LSCA) Grant
    Proposal, 17
Lincoln Trail Libraries System (LTLS), 25, 33, 69, 83
LOTUS program, 18, 21
Lovington Public Library District, 97–99

Management information system (MIS), 59–60
Marrowbone Public Library District, 97–99
Materials Availability Survey, 21
Median age of collections, 22
Median Age Tally Sheet, 72, 73, 78
Metro Music Division, 33
Montana State University, Division Report for, 40
Mosher, Paul, 11, 57, 58
"Multi-type Library Collection Planning in Alaska: a
    Conspectus-Based Approach" (Stephens), 58

Narrative summary, 46–47, 50–53
National Library of Medicine classification scheme,
    18 33
Nebraska Library Commission, 70, 73, 78, 81
Nebraska Library Commission Advisory Council, 81

New Jersey, Krueger Method in, 26
New Jersey Association of Library Assistants, 26
New Jersey Library Association, 26
New York Metropolitan Reference and Research
    Library Agency (METRO), 33
New Zealand, fiction assessment in, 69
Nicholls State University (NSU) Library, 43–47, 44
        background of, 43–44
        collection assessment narrative summary for,
            46–47, 50–53
        conclusion and recommendations, 47
        introduction of collection assessment
            objectives and training at, 44–46
        objectives of, 44
        problem statement of, 43
Non-Fiction Overview Chart, 88, 89
North American Collections Inventory Project (NCIP),
    11–12
Northwest Canadian Studies Consortium, 58
Northwest Conspectus, 58
Northwest Regional Cooperative, 26

Output Measures for Public Libraries, 21
Overview charts, 88–90
"Ownership versus access" of library materials, 7–8

Pacific Northwest Collection Development (PNCD)
    Program, 31, 32
Pacific Northwest Conspectus. See WLN Conspectus
    (formerly Pacific Northwest Conspectus)
Parlin-Intersoll Library, 22
Peoria Heights Public Library, 19–21
Peoria Public Library, 19, 21
Psychology collection (sample narrative study), 47, 50

Random sampling and availability of the collection, 20
Report & Recommendations for Cooperative
    Collection Development Acticities in the Illinois
    Valley Library System (Schmidt), 22
Research and Resource Library Directors, 59
Research Libraries Group (RLC), Collection
    Management and Development Committee of, 11

Research Libraries Group (RLC) Conspectus, 11–12,
    22, 31, 45, 94, 96
Resource Sharing Alliance (RSA), 86
Rolling Prairie Library System, 17–18, 21, 97
Rosenberg, Betty, 84
Rural libraries
        cooperative collection management among,
            97–99
        effects of fiction assessment on, 83–86

Schmidt, Geri, 18, 21, 22
Self-nomination of strengths method, 16
Shelf list measurement, 20
Southwestern Connecticut Library Council, 26–27
Sparta Public Library, 101–2
Stam, David H., 11
Stephens, Dennis, 57, 58

Three Rivers Regional Library Service System
    Cooperative Collection Development Project, 26

University of Alaska (Fairbanks), collection
    assessment for, 39

Virtual library, 7–8

Weech, Terry, 22
"WLN BCL3 Collection Service," 45
WLN Collection Analysis Report, 33
        worksheet examples and, 35–42
WLN Collection Assessment Manual, 44–46, 70, 78, 81
WLN Conspectus (formerly Pacific Northwest
    Conspectus), 22, 25, 29–68, 97, 101
        Alaska Collection Development Project and,
            57–60
        database, 59
        fiction assessment and, 69, 70, 73, 80, 81
        information uses, 33–34
        in non-automated environment, 43–55. See
            also Nicholls State University (NSU) Library
        structure of, 31–32
WLN Conspectus Software Version 5.0, 33